BIBLE STORY SNAPSHOTS

Dr. Scott Hanks

ISBN: 978-1-941772-48-5

COPYRIGHT © 2019 BY

1781 E. 800 ROAD
LAWRENCE, KS 66049
WWW.MERCYANDTRUTHMINISTRY.COM

A ministry of Heritage Baptist Church

Printed in the United States of America

OLD TESTAMENT

ACKNOWLEDGMENTS

I appreciate the ladies who helped with the countless hours of editing and proofreading: Stacia Hanks, Joy Smith, Stephanie Stumfoll, Lani Benton, and Carrie Selim.

DEDICATION

I would like to dedicate this book to a man who was my best friend in ministry until the Lord took him home on August 19, 2018. Dr. Rick Dawson began in ministry as a school teacher, youth pastor, and an assistant pastor. In 1984, he started the Victory Baptist Church in Carterville, Illinois, and ministered there for 26 years. The Lord then led him to the Clearview Baptist Church in Heber Springs, Arkansas, where he pastored for 10 years before God took him home to Heaven. For the last 12 years of his life, the Lord used him to challenge, strengthen, and encourage me in the ministry. I am grateful for his friendship and godly influence in my life

Introduction

Although *Bible Story Snapshots* from the Old Testament was designed to be used for family altar, it is also a great curriculum for a Christian School Bible class, a Sunday school class, a one-on-one discipleship Bible study, or even a group Bible study. It can also be used for ideas for seed thoughts for messages or devotionals. The **"story to tell"** is a short summary of the Bible story that covers a few verses, or a couple of chapters in Scripture. The **"truths to teach"** are thought-provoking truths that can open up several doors to teach different topics, thoughts, or ideas. These simple truths just scratch the surface of the principles that could be taught from the story. The **"questions to ask"** can be used for a quick review of the story. The answers to the questions can be found in the three introductory verses or in the paragraph summary of the story. The questions are meant to be easily answered from the scripture or summary.

Often the main stories in the Old Testament, such as, Daniel and the lion's den, or Jonah and the whale, are preached and taught, and many of the shorter stories are unfamiliar. *Bible Story Snapshots* takes a look at some of these seemingly small or incidental stories that are packed full of principles to be applied to the Christian life.

It is my prayer that this collection of 365 *Bible Story Snapshots* from the Old Testament is as enjoyable for you to study, as it was for me.

- Scott Hanks

Contents

Genesis .... Page 6

Exodus - Deuteronomy .... Page 49

Joshua - Ruth .... Page 91

I Samuel .... Page 123

II Samuel .... Page 169

I Kings .... Page 210

II Kings .... Page 250

I & II Chronicles .... Page 289

Ezra - Malachi .... Page 329

The Beginning
Genesis 1:1-3
Further Study: Genesis 1:1-31

The first story of the Bible is that of God creating all things. Genesis 1:1 says, "In the beginning God created the heaven and the earth." The first verse of the Bible is the key to every Christian's faith. All the universe was created by God. The word "create" means to cause to exist. He made something out of nothing. We, by faith, believe God created everything in six days, and on the seventh day, God rested. Hebrews 11:3 says, "Through faith we understand that the worlds were framed by the word of God, so that things which are seen were not made of things which do appear."

---

1. Who created the Heavens and the earth? *God*

2. What does the word "create" mean? *to cause to exist,*

3. What causes us to believe God created the Heavens and the earth? *Faith*

4. God made something out of what? *out of nothing*

5. How much of the Heavens and the earth did God create? *all of it*

> **Important Truths:**
>
> God is the beginning of everything.
>
> God created everything.
>
> God's beginning and His creation of all are accepted by us, through faith.

Six Days of Creation

Genesis 1:29-31

(Study: Genesis 1:1-31)

Genesis chapter one gives us the historical account of God creating the heaven and the earth. On the first day, God created light. On the second day, God created the heavens. On the third day, God created the earth. On the fourth day, God created the sun, moon, and stars. On the fifth day, God created fish and fowl. On the sixth day, God created land animals and man. When God was finished creating the world, He said, "It was very good." God is the Creator of the universe and He did it in six literal days, and rested on the seventh.

---

1. What did God create on the first and second day? light, heavens

2. What did God create on the third and fourth day? earth, sun, moon and stars

3. What did God create on the fifth and sixth day? fish & fowl, land animals + man

4. Everything that God had made was what? Very good

5. How many days did it take for God to create the world? 6

Important Truths:

God created the world in six literal days.

Everything that God created was "very good."

God sees everything that He has made.

Satan's Temptation
Genesis 3:1-3
(Study: Genesis 3:1-15)

Satan, by way of a serpent, tempted Eve to disobey God. God told Adam and Eve not to eat from the tree of knowledge of good and evil. Satan's very first statement of deception was "Yea, hath God said." He cast doubt on the Word of God in order to get Eve to disobey God. The serpent was called subtle, which means cunning or crafty. Satan is a master deceiver of both the lost and saved. Romans 5:12 says, "Wherefore, as by one man sin entered into the world, and death by sin; and so death passed upon all men, for that all have sinned:"

---

1. What reptile did Satan use to deceive Eve?

2. What was Satan's first question to Eve?

3. From what tree did God tell Adam and Eve not to eat?

4. What does the word "subtle" mean?

5. What are some ways that Satan will try to tempt you?

Important Truths:

Satan's deception is to always make sin not look so bad.

Satan will always cast doubt on the Word of God.

Satan will always do what he has always done, tempt you to sin.

Fall of Man

Genesis 3:6-8

(Study: Genesis 3:1-19)

Adam and Eve were placed in the Garden of Eden and God told them not to eat of the tree of the knowledge of good and evil. They could eat of any other tree except for that one. Satan knew this and tempted Eve to eat of the fruit of that tree. He tempted her with the lust of the flesh, the lust of the eyes, and the pride of life. Through deceit and lies, Satan convinced Eve to eat of the fruit and then she gave it to her husband. Their fall brought sin into the world, and death because of sin (Romans 5:12).

---

1. Who tempted Eve to eat the fruit?

2. To whom did Eve give the forbidden fruit?

3. Why did Eve desire the fruit?

4. What two things did Adam and Eve's sin bring into the world?

5. What did Satan use to trick Eve?

Important Truths:

Satan will question the truth of the Word of God.

Satan will appeal to our senses.

Satan will appeal to the lust of our flesh, lust of our eyes, and our pride.

Cain and Abel's Offering
Genesis 4:3-5
(Study: Genesis 4:1-5)

Cain and Abel brought offerings unto the Lord. Cain brought an offering of the fruit of the ground, and Abel brought the firstling of his flock. Abel's offering was acceptable to the Lord and Cain's was not. The reason Abel's offering was pleasing to the Lord was because it was a blood sacrifice. The Lord had respect unto Abel and his offering. Cain's fruit of the ground showed his own works, while Abel offered what God wanted, which was a blood sacrifice. The Lord did not have respect unto Cain and his offering.

---

1. What was Cain's offering?

2. What was Abel's offering?

3. Why did God have respect unto Abel's offering and not Cain's?

4. What was Cain's reaction when his offering was not accepted?

5. Cain's fruit of the ground illustrates man's own what?

Important Truths:

"…without shedding of blood is no remission."

Cain did a right thing, the wrong way.

Cain and Abel both made a choice.

Cain Murders Abel

Genesis 4:8-10

(Study: Genesis 4:1-15)

Cain and Abel each brought sacrifices to God. Cain's offering was the fruit of the ground, while Abel's was the firstling of his flock. Cain was angry that God accepted Abel's offering and not his own, and he killed his brother while they were in the field one day. God knew that Cain had killed his brother Abel, but gave him an opportunity to repent by asking him, "Where is Abel thy brother?" Cain's response showed no remorse when he said, "Am I my brother's keeper?" God punished him by making him a fugitive and vagabond in the earth for the rest of his life.

---

1. Where was Cain when he killed Abel?

2. What cried from the ground telling God that Abel was dead?

3. What was God's punishment on Cain for killing Abel?

4. How did Cain lie to God?

5. What caused Cain to kill his brother?

> **Important Truths:**
>
> Jesus compared the sin of murder with hating your brother.
>
> "Whoso sheddeth man's blood, by man shall his blood be shed."
>
> You cannot hide your sin from God.

Enoch Walked with God

Genesis 5:22-24
(Study: Genesis 5:18-24)

Enoch is the first one of only a few to be mentioned as one who "walked with God." The last people before Enoch that were mentioned to have walked with God were Adam and Eve (Genesis 3:8). Encoh only lived on the earth for 365 years because "God took him." He, like Elijah, never experienced a natural death because God translated them to Heaven while they were still alive. It is interesting that Enoch did not walk with God until "after" his son Methuselah was born. Methuselah still holds the record for the longest living person. He lived to be 969 years old.

1. When did Enoch start walking with God?

2. What happened to Enoch because he walked with God?

3. How long did Enoch's son Methuselah live?

4. Which two men in the Bible never died?

5. How old was Enoch when God took him?

Important Truths:

We walk with God through prayer and Bible study.

Walking with God pleases Him.

Faith is key to walking with God.

Noah Found Grace

Genesis 6:7-9

(Study: Genesis 6:5-13)

God saw that man was wicked, violent, and corrupt, and that every imagination of the thoughts of his heart was evil continually. Because of man's sin, God decided to destroy the earth with a flood. Yet, in His mercy, God would provide an ark of safety for those who would believe. The person God chose to build this ark was Noah, because Noah found grace in the eyes of the Lord. The word grace means favour. Noah was favorable to God because he was a just man, he was perfect in his generation, and he walked with God.

---

1. With Whom did Noah walk?

2. What type of man was Noah?

3. Noah found what in the eyes of the Lord?

4. What does the word "grace" mean?

5. Why would God destroy the earth with a flood?

Important Truths:

The penalty for sin was the flood.

The mercy and grace of God was providing the ark.

Noah was used of God because he was favorable to God.

Noah Builds an Ark

Genesis 6:13-15
(Study: Genesis 6:8-22)

God told Noah to build an ark that was about 450 feet long, 75 feet wide, and 45 feet tall. It was to have one door and three floors. Noah was to bring into the ark two of every sort of living thing, both male and female. Along with him and his family, he would also have food for all. Noah did "according to all that God commanded him." While Noah prepared the ark, he preached righteousness (II Peter 2:5). Even though God was longsuffering to those present in Noah's day, only Noah, his wife, his three sons, and their wives survived.

1. How big was the ark?

2. How many doors were in the ark?

3. God said He would destroy the earth because the earth was filled with what?

4. How many of each animal were brought in the ark?

5. How many people were in the ark?

Important Truths:

Noah, by faith, did what God commanded even though there had never been rain.

There was only one door into the ark, and there is only one way to Heaven.

Noah was a preacher of righteousness.

Noah and the Flood

Genesis 7:16-18
(Study: Genesis 7:1-24)

After Noah built the ark, God told him and his family and the animals to go inside the ark. The Lord sent the animals, two by two, male and female, to Noah, to place in the ark. For seven days, they waited inside the ark until the Lord shut the door. In God's mercy, He left the door open to the ark seven more days after Noah had preached for 120 years. Then, the Lord caused it to rain forty days and forty nights so that the waters flooded the world until the highest mountains were covered. Every man and animal outside the ark died.

---

1. How many days was Noah in the ark before the door was shut?

2. Who shut the door to the ark?

3. How many days and nights did it rain?

4. Who brought the animals to Noah?

5. How many people died that were outside of the ark?

Important Truths:

God leaves an open door for all to be saved.

One day God will shut the door either by death or His second coming.

Only eight were in the ark. The majority of mankind is lost.

The Rainbow

Genesis 9:12-14
(Study: Genesis 9:1-17)

After the flood, God told Noah and his sons, "Be fruitful, and multiply, and replenish the earth." God promised Noah that He would never destroy the earth again with a flood. He promised a token as a reminder of that covenant. The rainbow that we see in the sky after it rains is that token of God's promise. God said, "The bow shall be in the cloud; and I will look upon it, that I may remember the everlasting covenant between God and every living creature of all flesh that is upon the earth."

---

1. What did God tell Noah to do after he came off the ark?

2. What did God promise that He would never do again?

3. What was the token of God's promise?

4. What is a covenant?

5. What does God remember when He sees a rainbow?

Important Truths:

A rainbow should remind us that God always keeps His promises.

God is in control of nature.

The flood reminds us of God's judgment, and the rainbow reminds us of God's mercy.

Tower of Babel

Genesis 11:3-5
(Study: Genesis 11:1-9)

In Genesis 9:1, God told Noah that man was to "replenish" (to fill) the earth. At the Tower of Babel, the people said, "let us build us a city and a tower, whose top may reach unto heaven; and let us make us a name, lest we be scattered abroad upon the face of the whole earth." God was not pleased with their pride and disobedience and so He confounded their language. When they could not understand one another's speech, it forced them to stop building and separate. The word "Babel" means confusion, for it was there that God confused their languages.

1. The people made a tower in hopes of making what?

2. How were they disobeying God by making a tower?

3. What did they use to make their tower?

4. What does the word "Babel" mean?

5. What did God do to scatter these people throughout the earth?

Important Truths:

We should not try to make a name for ourselves.

The Lord sees everything we are doing.

The Lord directs man's steps.

Abraham's Blessing
Genesis 12:1-3
(Study: Genesis 12:1-9)

From Abraham would come the nation of Israel. Long before Abraham and Sarah had any children, God promised him that He would make of him a great nation and name. The generations of Abraham would come to be called the children of Israel. God said that all those that bless Israel would be blessed, and all those that cursed Israel would be cursed. At age seventy-five, Abraham came into the land of Canaan and the Lord said to him, "Unto thy seed will I give this land" (Genesis 12:7).

1. From whom did God tell Abraham to separate?

2. What two things would be "great" about Abraham?

3. What did God tell Abraham he would be?

4. Who would be blessed because of Abraham?

5. What nation did Abraham father?

Important Truths:

God's blessing is upon the nation of Israel!

God blesses those who bless Israel and God curses those who curse Israel.

Abraham's personal blessing was dependent upon separation.

For We Be Brethren
Genesis 13:7-9
(Study: Genesis 13:5-13)

Lot was Abraham's nephew. Both of them came into the land of Canaan and God blessed them with large flocks and herds of animals. In time, Abraham and Lot's herdsmen began to strive with one another. Abraham told Lot, "Let there be no strife…for we be brethren. Is not the whole land before thee? separate thyself, I pray thee, from me: if thou wilt take the left hand, then I will go to the right; or if thou depart to the right hand, then I will go to the left." So the two of them separated from one another. Abraham dwelt in the land of Canaan, and Lot chose to pitch his tent toward Sodom.

1. The strife was between whom?

2. How were Abraham and Lot related?

3. What was the reason Abraham gave to Lot for not wanting strife between them?

4. Lot pitched his tent toward what city?

5. Who was also in the land and could see Abraham and Lot's strife?

Important Truths:

Brethren should not strive with each other.

Abraham acted as the bigger Christian and offered Lot his choice of place, to fix the problem.

"Substance" (money) often causes strife.

Lot Taken Captive

Genesis 14:12-14
(Study: Genesis 14:1-16)

Lot was dwelling in Sodom at the time that a war broke out. There were five kings fighting against four kings. The king of Sodom was on the losing side and Lot was taken captive and all that he had. Lot would not have been taken captive if he would not have been living in Sodom. Uncle Abraham came to Lot's rescue with 318 of his own trained servants. At a time when five kings could not stand up against four, Abraham did, and brought back all the captives and spoil that was taken, along with Lot.

---

1. Where did Lot dwell?

2. How many kings fought against each other?

3. How many of Abraham's servants fought?

4. Which three people were confederate with Abraham?

5. Who told Abraham that Lot was taken captive?

Important Truths:

Lot should have never been in Sodom (the world).

God is bigger than any army.

We should help brothers who are taken captive by the world, like Abraham helped Lot.

Abraham Intercedes
Genesis 18:23-25
(Study: Genesis 18:16-33)

The Lord came down and talked with Abraham and told him that He was about to destroy Sodom and Gomorrah "because their sin is very grievous." Abraham knew that his nephew Lot and his family lived there, and began to plead with God not to destroy it. Abraham asked God to spare the place if fifty righteous people could be found therein. God agreed to his request. However, Abraham continued asking for the sake of 45, then 40, 30, 20, and finally 10. God said, "I will not destroy it for ten's sake."

---

1. Abraham said God was the what of all the earth?

2. Who did Abraham ask God not to destroy with the wicked?

3. Why was God going to destroy Sodom and Gomorrah?

4. For the sake of how many did God say He would spare Sodom?

5. What relative of Abraham's dwelt in Sodom?

Important Truths:

God knew Abraham.

God answered Abraham's requests.

Interceding to God for others is important.

Sodom & Gomorrah
Genesis 19:24-26
(Study: Genesis 19:1-26)

God sent two angels to warn Lot and his family to get out of Sodom before it was destroyed. Lot tried to convince his sons in law to leave, but they did not take him seriously and stayed. The angels had to take Lot, his wife, and his two daughters by the hand and lead them out of the city. God rained fire and brimstone upon the cities of Sodom and Gomorrah for their wickedness. Lot's wife became a pillar of salt because she disobeyed the angel's command to not look back.

1. What did the Lord rain upon Sodom and Gomorrah?

2. Who in Lot's family did the angels lead out of Sodom?

3. Lot's wife was turned into what?

4. Why did she die?

5. Why were the cities destroyed?

Important Truths:

Lot should not have been in the world.

Sodom was characterized by the sin of homosexuality.

We should never look back to the world.

Abraham's Half Truth

Genesis 20:10-12
(Study: Genesis 20:1-18)

After God destroyed Sodom and Gomorrah, Abraham and his wife traveled south to a place called Gerar. While there, the king of Gerar, Abimelech, took Abraham's wife as his own, thinking that Sarah was his sister not his wife. Because Abraham thought that the men of that place would kill him in order to take his wife, he told them that she was his sister. This is a half truth because they had the same father, but not the same mother. God protected Abraham and reproved Abimelech for taking his wife. Abimelech returned Sarah to Abraham.

---

1. Why did Abraham lie concerning his wife?

2. Where was Abraham when he lied?

3. What was the name of the king that took Abraham's wife?

4. How was Sarah Abraham's sister?

5. What did Abraham say "is not in this place?"

Important Truths:

We are to fear God and not man.

A half-truth is still a lie.

The Lord protects His own.

Birth of Isaac

Genesis 21:1-3
(Study: Genesis 21:1-12)

God promised Abraham and Sarah that they would have a child. That promise came to pass when Abraham was one hundred years old and Sarah was ninety. The child that was born was named Isaac. Fourteen years earlier, while waiting for this promised child, Abraham took Hagar, their Egyptian servant, and had a son named Ishmael. God, however, said that through Isaac would Abraham's seed be called. Isaac's name means laughter for which he was called because Sarah laughed at the thought at having a child in her old age.

1. How old was Abraham when Isaac was born?

2. What was the name of Abraham's two sons?

3. What was the name of Ishmael's mother?

4. How old was Abraham when Ishmael was born?

5. What does Isaac's name mean?

Important Truths:

We should wait on God instead of taking things into our own hands.

God can do the impossible.

God always keeps His promises.

Offering up of Isaac

Genesis 22:1-3

(Study: Genesis 22:1-19)

God put Abraham to the test to see if he feared and loved Him more than his son Isaac. The word "tempt" in Genesis 22:1 means to test or prove. When God told Abraham to take his son Isaac and offer him up as a burnt offering, he obeyed. On the way up the mountain, Isaac asked, "Where is the lamb?" Abraham believed God and said, "God will provide himself a lamb." Abraham's love for God surpassed his love for his son Isaac. After Abraham proved his obedience, God supplied a ram caught in a thicket to be sacrificed instead of Isaac.

1. What mountain did Abraham go up on to sacrifice Isaac?

2. What does it mean when the Bible says, "God did tempt Abraham"?

3. What did God provide as a sacrifice in place of Isaac?

4. What did Abraham say when God called his name?

5. Whom did Abraham love the most, God, or his son Isaac?

Important Truths:

God will put us to the test.

We should want to give God what we love the most.

Jesus was the Lamb that was sacrificed for us.

Bride for Isaac

Genesis 24:2-4

(Study: Genesis 24:1-67)

Abraham was old and concerned that his son Isaac would have the wife God wanted for him. Abraham did not want his son marrying a Canaanite, nor did he want his son to leave the Promised Land to go back to his kindred to find a wife. Abraham sent his eldest servant back to Mesopotamia, where his kindred lived, to find a wife for Isaac. Upon arriving at the city of Nahor, he prayed by a well, and the Lord sent a young virgin named Rebekah. She gave the servant water and drew for his ten camels. Rebekah went back with the servant and married Isaac.

---

1. Whom did Abraham not want Isaac to marry?

2. Where did Abraham not want Isaac to leave?

3. Who was Isaac's wife?

4. Who brought Isaac a bride?

5. In what city did Rebekah live?

Important Truths:

Christians should not marry unbelievers.

God has someone "appointed" for marriage.

Parents are concerned about whom their child will marry.

Esau's Birthright

Genesis 25:29-31
(Study: Genesis 25:19-34)

Isaac and Rebekah were married twenty years before God allowed Rebekah to bear twins. Esau was the oldest and was a hunter and man of the field. Jacob was a plain man dwelling in tents. One day, Esau came from the field and was so faint he thought he was going to die. He asked Jacob to give him something to eat, and Jacob said he would, if Esau sold him his birthright. The birthright gave an extra portion of the family inheritance to the oldest. Esau did not esteem his birthright important and sold it for a bowl of soup.

---

1. Esau was a cunning what?

2. Jacob was what kind of man?

3. What was a birthright?

4. For what did Esau sell his birthright?

5. What did the scripture say Esau's name would be called?

Important Truths:

Some things are not for sale.

Don't make life changing decisions under pressure.

Brothers should take care of brothers.

Isaac's Lie

Genesis 26:7-9
(Study: Genesis 26:6-14)

There was a famine in the land and Isaac and Rebekah went to a city called Gerar, which had a king named Abimelech. While there, the men of the place asked Isaac if Rebekah was his wife, and he told them she was his sister. He feared that they would kill him and take his wife, so he lied to them. One day the king looked out a window and saw Isaac and Rebekah together and realized they were truly married. He called Isaac to him and asked, "How saidst thou, She is my sister? Isaac said, "Because I said, Lest I die for her." After the truth was brought out, the Lord blessed Isaac.

1. What was Isaac's lie?

2. Why did he lie about Rebekah being his wife?

3. Who was the king of Gerar?

4. What happened to Isaac after the truth was brought out?

5. What caused Isaac to go to Gerar?

Important Truths:

There is never a good reason to lie.

The fear of man bringeth a snare.

God blesses telling the truth.

Jacob Steals the Blessing

Genesis 27:34-36

(Study: Genesis 27:1-46)

Isaac calls Esau and tells him "Behold now, I am old, I know not the day of my death:...make me savoury meat, such as I love, and bring it to me, that I may eat; that my soul may bless thee before I die." Rebekah hears this and tells Jacob to do this so he can receive the blessing instead of Esau. Jacob brings the venison to Isaac, claiming to be Esau. Isaac blesses Jacob thinking it is Esau, his firstborn. Esau comes in shortly after Jacob leaves his father's presence to give his father venison and receive the blessing. He soon found out that Jacob not only took his birthright, but now his blessing. Esau hated his brother and wanted to kill him.

---

1. What two things did Jacob take from Esau his brother?

2. Who told Jacob to steal Esau's blessing?

3. Esau wanted to do what to Jacob for stealing the blessing?

4. To whom did Jacob lie?

5. Who said, "Bless me, even me also"?

> **Important Truths:**
>
> Parents should not show partiality.
>
> Children should not lie to their parents.
>
> A parent's blessing should be important to a child.

A Wife for Jacob
Genesis 27:44-46
(Study: Genesis 28:1-10)

Jacob had just stolen the blessing from Esau, and Esau wanted to kill him. Rebekah came to her husband Isaac and said, "I am weary of my life because of the daughters of Heth." She did not want her son Jacob to marry one of the Canaanite women. Isaac sent Jacob to Padan-aram, Rebekah's birthplace, to find a wife. Esau had married two Hittite women, "which were a grief of mind unto Isaac and to Rebekah" (Genesis 26:35). Jacob obeyed his parents and went to Padan-aram to find a wife.

1. What was a grief of mind to Isaac and Rebekah?

2. Who said that if Jacob married a Canaanite "what good shall my life do me"?

3. Where did Isaac send Jacob to find a wife?

4. Did Jacob obey his parents?

5. Who said, "I am weary of my life"?

Important Truths:

Your choice for marriage will affect your family.

Never look to the world for a spouse.

Follow a parent's advice concerning marriage.

Jacob's Dream
Genesis 28:13-15
(Study: Genesis 28:10-22)

Jacob obeyed his father and mother and headed to Padan-aram to find himself a wife. While traveling he laid down one night and had a dream of the angels of God ascending and descending on a ladder between the earth and Heaven. God stood above the ladder and promised Jacob that the land he was on would be given to him and his proceeding generations, and that his families would be in number as the dust of the earth. He also told him that He would not leave him, and that Jacob would come back again to this land. When Jacob awoke, he called the name of the place Bethel, which means house of God.

---

1. What would Jacob's seed be like?

2. In Jacob's seed would all the families of the earth be what?

3. What does Bethel mean?

4. Who spoke to Jacob in his dream?

5. What did God promise to give Jacob?

Important Truths:

Israel is God's chosen people.

God meets with us at the House of God.

Canaan land belongs to Israel.

Jacob Loved Rachel
Genesis 29:18-20
(Study: Genesis 29:1-35)

Jacob came to the land of the East and met Rachel at a well. Rachel was the daughter of Laban, who was the brother to Jacob's mother Rebekah. Jacob went to live and work at Laban's house. Laban asked him what his wages should be, and Jacob agreed to work for seven years in order to marry Rachel. Because Jacob loved Rachel so much, the seven years "seemed unto him but a few days." The day came for him to marry Rachel, but Laban tricked Jacob and gave him his other daughter Leah. Jacob was not satisfied with Leah, so he also married Rachel because he loved her more. He ended up working seven more years in order to marry Rachel.

1. Who was Laban?

2. Where did Jacob meet Rachel?

3. How many years did he work for Rachel?

4. Who did Jacob marry before Rachel?

5. Who was Leah?

Important Truths:

Jacob was willing to work and wait to marry.

Jacob reaped being deceived because of his practice of deception of Esau.

God wants a man to marry one woman for life.

Blessed for Jacob's Sake

Genesis 30:25-27
(Study: Genesis 27:25-43)

After Joseph was born, Jacob wanted to go back to his homeland. Jacob had worked for Laban for fourteen years. In that time, Laban could see all that God had done for him because of Jacob's working for him. When Jacob asked to leave, Laban said he would pay Jacob whatever he asked if he would stay. It was worth whatever the cost, to continue having God's blessing on him and his household. Laban told Jacob, "I have learned by experience that the LORD hath blessed me for thy sake."

1. What happened that caused Jacob to want to go back home to his own country?

2. How many years did Jacob serve Laban?

3. Why did the Lord bless Laban?

4. What did Jacob tell Laban that he knew?

5. Did Jacob stay and work for Laban?

Important Truths:

Who does God bless for your sake?

Would people pay whatever to keep you as a worker?

We should pay whatever the cost to have the blessing of the Lord on our lives.

Jacob Wrestles

Genesis 32:24-26
(Study: Genesis 32:23-32)

Jacob begins his trek homeward with his family after leaving Laban. He sends word to his brother Esau that he is coming home and finds out that Esau is coming to meet him with 400 men. Jacob is afraid and sends his family ahead of him so that he can be alone to pray. Jacob wrestles until morning with a Man that he considers to be God. When this Man from God begins to leave, Jacob refuses to let Him go unless He blesses him. Jacob is blessed and God changes his name to Israel.

---

1. How long did Jacob wrestle?

2. What was put out of joint while Jacob wrestled?

3. Jacob would not let the Man from God go unless He did what?

4. Why was Jacob afraid?

5. Who was with Jacob when he wrestled the Man from God?

Important Truths:

How badly do you want God's blessing?

We should get alone to meet with God.

It is always best to go to God when we are afraid.

Go Up to Bethel
Genesis 35:1-3
(Study: Genesis 35:1-15)

The word "Beth-el" means house of God. It was the place that Jacob first met with God when fleeing from Esau his brother. God told Jacob to go back to Bethel with his entire family. Before Jacob and his family went up to Bethel, He told them to put away the strange gods, be clean, and to change their garments. Jacob's family gave him all the strange gods and he buried them under an oak in Shechem. Jacob journeyed to Bethel in Canaan land and built there an altar unto the Lord. It was there that God appeared unto Jacob and blessed him.

---

1. What does Bethel mean?

2. Where was Bethel?

3. What three things did Jacob tell his family to do before going to Bethel?

4. What did God do for Jacob at Bethel?

5. What did Jacob do with the strange gods?

Important Truths:

Prepare to go to the house of God.

Blessings come from going to the house of God.

Do not miss services at the house of God.

Joseph the Favorite

Genesis 37:2-4
(Study: Genesis 37:1-27)

Joseph was the eleventh of the twelve sons of Jacob. Jacob "loved Joseph more than all his children." Jacob showed this superior love to Joseph by giving him a coat of many colors. Unfortunately, this favoritism toward Joseph caused his other brothers to envy and hate Joseph. Joseph's brothers were bothered so much by their father's love to Joseph that they could not speak peaceably with him and even spoke of killing him. Joseph was seventeen when he received special attention from his father and hatred from his brothers.

---

1. What did Jacob give to Joseph?

2. What two feelings did Joseph's brothers have toward him?

3. Jacob showed what toward Joseph?

4. How old was Joseph when his brothers could not talk to him peaceably?

5. Why did Jacob love Joseph more than all his children?

Important Truths:

We should not show respect of persons.

We should not have hatred toward people.

Parents should not show favoritism.

Joseph's Dreams
Genesis 37:8-10
(Study: Genesis 37:5-20)

Joseph dreamed two dreams and told them to his brothers. The first dream he dreamed was about he and his brothers binding sheaves in the field. His sheaf stood up in the field and all his brother's sheaves made obeisance to his sheaf. His second dream was that the sun, moon, and stars made obeisance to him. These dreams caused his brothers to hate him more and his father to rebuke him. Little did they know that these dreams would come true when he became the governor of Egypt. Joseph's brothers called him a "dreamer," but his dreams would become a reality.

---

1. How many dreams did Joseph dream?

2. In both dreams, Joseph's family did what to him?

3. When did Joseph's dreams come true?

4. How did Joseph's brothers feel toward him for his dreams?

5. Who rebuked Joseph for his dreams?

Important Truths:

Joseph's dreams were given to him by God.

People will sometimes hate you for your dreams.

There are things you ought to dream about doing for God.

Joseph Sold into Egypt
Genesis 37:26-28
(Study: Genesis 37:20-36)

Joseph's brothers were out taking care of the flocks in Dothan. Jacob sent Joseph to check on his brothers and the flocks. While Joseph was coming to his brothers, they conspired to kill him. They took Joseph and stripped him of his coat of many colors and threw him into a pit. Judah told his brothers that they should not kill him because he was their brother. They decided to sell him for twenty pieces of silver to the Midianite merchantmen that were passing by. Joseph's brothers took his coat and dipped it in blood so that his father would think some animal had killed him.

---

1. Whose idea was it to sell Joseph?

2. Who bought Joseph?

3. For how much was Joseph sold?

4. Where did the Midianites take Joseph?

5. How did Joseph's brothers convince their father that Joseph was dead?

Important Truths:

Hatred can cause you to do bad things.

Bad things can happen to good people.

God is able to protect us from evil men.

Joseph in Potiphar's House
Genesis 39:3-5
(Study: Genesis 39:1-6)

Joseph was sold into Egypt as a slave to a man named Potiphar. Potiphar was the captain of the guard, an officer of Pharaoh, king of Egypt. As Joseph served Potiphar "the Lord made all that he did to prosper." Potiphar noticed that the Lord was with Joseph and that all that he did, prospered, so he made him overseer over all his house. "The LORD blessed the Egyptian's house for Joseph's sake." Joseph was a blessing and help to Potiphar because he was a goodly person, had a servant's heart, and the Lord was with him.

1. Who was with Joseph?

2. The Lord made all that Joseph did to what?

3. Why did the Lord bless Potiphar?

4. In what two places did the Lord bless Potiphar?

5. Why was Joseph a prosperous man?

Important Truths:

We should serve God even in unfavorable conditions.

The Lord being with us and prospering go hand in hand.

Can we be trusted with "all" that a person has?

Joseph Tempted
Genesis 39:7-9
(Study: Genesis 39:7-23)

Joseph was sold into Egypt as a slave to a man named Potiphar. In the process of time, his master's wife desired to have Joseph as her own. Joseph knew that it would be a sin to commit adultery and told her no. She did not like being rejected by Joseph and every day she spoke to him to try to tempt him to sin. Joseph would not hearken to her "to lie by her, or to be with her." One day, while Joseph was doing his business in the house she caught him and said, "Lie with me." Joseph "left his garment in her hand, and fled, and got him out."

---

1. Who cast her eyes upon Joseph?

2. Joseph said he could not sin against whom?

3. How often was Joseph tempted by her?

4. What sin was Potiphar's wife asking Joseph to commit?

5. When fleeing temptation, what did Joseph leave behind?

Important Truths:
Learn to say "NO."
Run from temptation!
All sin is against God.

Joseph in Prison
Genesis 39:20-22
(Study: Genesis 39:7-23)

Joseph was tempted to commit adultery with Potiphar's wife, but said no. Potiphar's wife falsely accused Joseph and her husband put him in prison. God looked after Joseph and gave him favor in the sight of the keeper of the prison. The keeper of the prison committed to Joseph's hand all the prisoners, and did not look to see what Joseph did with them. Just like the Lord was with Joseph in Potiphar's house, so He was with Joseph in prison. God made everything that Joseph did to prosper. Even in Joseph's affliction in prison, God was merciful to him.

---

1. Who falsely accused Joseph?

2. In whose sight did God give Joseph favor?

3. What was committed to Joseph?

4. God made everything Joseph did to what?

5. "The LORD was with Joseph, and shewed him" what?

Important Truths:

God can give us favor with man.

Prison was God's path to the palace for Joseph.

God is always everywhere with us.

Joseph Interprets Dreams
Genesis 40:6-8
(Study: Genesis 40:1-23)

Joseph was in prison and put in charge of the prisoners. The king's butler and baker were put in the ward where Joseph was bound. One night, both the butler and baker dreamed dreams that troubled them. Joseph noticed they were sad and said to them, "Do not interpretations belong to God?" Joseph interpreted both of their dreams. The butler would return to serve Pharaoh, but the baker would hang to death. Three days later was Pharaoh's birthday, and just as Joseph interpreted their dreams, the dreams came true.

1. What two officers of the king were put in prison with Joseph?

2. Who did Joseph say could interpret dreams?

3. What did the butler's dream reveal?

4. What did the baker's dream reveal?

5. What event took place three days after the butler and baker dreamed?

Important Truths:

God is in control of even our sleep.

God uses people to give us help and direction.

God has an answer to every question.

Joseph Forgotten
Genesis 40:13-15
(Study: Genesis 41:1-13)

Joseph was used of God while in prison to interpret the dreams of the butler and baker. Joseph asked the butler to shew kindness to him and mention Joseph's name to Pharaoh when he was released. When the butler returned to his butlership, he forgot about Joseph. Two years later, Pharaoh had a dream that caused the butler to remember Joseph. The butler told Pharaoh that when he was in prison, there was a Hebrew young man that interpreted his dream, and it came to pass just like he said. Pharaoh quickly called for Joseph to see if he could interpret his dream.

---

1. Who forgot Joseph?

2. How many years did he forget him?

3. What caused the butler to remember Joseph?

4. What kindness did Joseph want from the butler?

5. What did Joseph do for the butler?

Important Truths:

People will not always return your kindness.

God's timing for Joseph was perfect.

People forget us, but God does not.

Joseph Made Ruler in Egypt
Genesis 41:38-40
(Study: Genesis 41:14-44)

Pharaoh had a dream that his magicians could not interpret. When the butler remembered that two years earlier Joseph had interpreted his dream in prison, he told Pharaoh. Joseph was brought to Pharaoh immediately and he told Joseph his two dreams. Joseph told Pharaoh, "What God is about to do he sheweth unto Pharaoh." Joseph interpreted the dreams and showed Pharaoh that there would be seven years of great plenty followed by seven years of great famine. Joseph told Pharaoh that he would need to appoint someone to collect and store food during the years of plenty so that Egypt did not perish during the years of famine. Pharaoh made Joseph that man to rule over Egypt.

---

1. What did Pharaoh see in Joseph?

2. Joseph would be second in command under whom?

3. Pharaoh said that Joseph was what two things?

4. Who told Pharaoh about Joseph?

5. How many years of famine would there be?

Important Truths:

Promotion comes from the Lord.

We should not forget those who have helped us.

The Christian has the answer the world needs.

Joseph's Two Sons
Genesis 41:50-52
(Study: Genesis 41:45-57)

God took Joseph out of prison and made him governor of Egypt. During the first seven years of plenty in Egypt, Joseph had two sons born. The firstborn he named Manasseh whose name means forgetting, and the second he named Ephraim meaning fruitful. Joseph was thirty years old when he stood before Pharaoh. From Joseph's youth, he went to a pit, to Potipher's house, to prison, and finally to the palace. In the naming of his sons, Joseph showed that he had to forget the past before he would ever be fruitful. God blessed Joseph beyond measure. Joseph would have never have become fruitful if he was bitter about his brothers selling him into Egypt and his having to endure the afflictions of prison.

---

1. How old was Joseph when he became governor?

2. What does Manasseh's name mean?

3. What does Ephraim's name mean?

4. What was the name of Joseph's wife?

5. Joseph could forget because he did not get what?

Important Truths:

Forgetting came before being fruitful.

Good always comes to those who do right.

Recognize God's hand of direction in your life.

Joseph's Dreams Come True
Genesis 42:7-9
(Study: Genesis 42:1-26)

Twenty years earlier Joseph dreamed that his brethren would bow down to him (Genesis 37:5-10). His brothers hated him for his dreams and scoffed at the idea that he would reign over them. They ridiculed Joseph by calling him a "dreamer." Before Joseph's brothers sold him into Egypt they contemplated killing him and said, "we shall see what will become of his dreams" (Genesis 37:20). Sure enough, they did see what became of Joseph's dreams, twenty years later. They came and bowed before Joseph seeking bread during the seven years of famine.

1. How many years did it take before Joseph's dreams came true?

2. When Joseph's brothers bowed before Joseph, did they know it was him?

3. What did Joseph remember when he saw his brothers?

4. For what did Joseph's brothers hate him?

5. During the famine, Joseph's brothers came and did what before him?

Important Truths:

Be careful not to think something could never happen.

Only time will reveal what God's will is.

People will ridicule your dreams.

Joseph Reveals Himself
Genesis 45:1-3
(Study: Genesis 45:1-15)

Joseph's brothers came to Egypt for food during the famine, but did not recognize Joseph. Upon their second visit to Egypt, Joseph reveals to them that he was Joseph whom they sold into Egypt. Joseph comforts his brothers and tells them, "it was not you that sent me hither, but God." Joseph tells his brothers to go back to Canaan and bring back his father and all that they have so that he can nourish them during the remaining five years of famine. After revealing himself to his brothers he wept, embraced, and talked with them.

1. Who sent Joseph into Egypt?

2. Who did Joseph want his brothers to bring back to Egypt?

3. How many years of famine were left?

4. Who was with Joseph when he revealed himself to his brothers?

5. Who heard Joseph weep?

Important Truths:

People are not in control of our future, God is.

Forgiveness can overcome the desire to retaliate.

Happy endings come from right living.

Joseph Knows His Place
Genesis 50:18-20
(Study: Genesis 50:15-26)

When Joseph's father died, his brothers thought that he would retaliate against them for selling him into Egypt. Joseph's brothers came and bowed before Joseph to seek forgiveness and mercy. Joseph reminded them that he was not in the place of God to give such a judgment against them. He told them what they meant for evil, God meant for good! He told them to not be afraid, but that he would nourish and take care of them and their families. Joseph's kind words were a comfort to his brothers. Joseph lived to be one hundred and ten and was put in a coffin in Egypt.

1. Why did Joseph's brothers think Joseph would be mean to them?

2. Who said, "Am I in the place of God?"

3. What Joseph's brothers meant for evil, God meant for what?

4. How long did Joseph live?

5. What comforted Joseph's brothers?

Important Truths:

What man means for evil, God can mean for good.

We should not put ourselves in the place of God.

Do not retaliate.

Israel's Bondage
Exodus 1:11-13
(Study: Exodus 1:1-22)

After Joseph and all his generation died, there arose a new king of Egypt which knew not Joseph. This new Pharaoh of Egypt put the children of Israel under hard bondage. He made them build the treasure cities of Pithom and Raamses. He made the Israelites' "lives bitter with hard bondage, in morter, and in brick." Making the children of Israel slaves did not satisfy the king of Egypt. He even killed their babies. He decreed to his people that they should cast every male child born to an Israelite into the river.

1. What cities did the Israelites build for Pharaoh?

2. Who afflicted the Israelites?

3. When did Pharaoh put the children of Israel under hard bondage?

4. How did the Egyptians kill every male Israelite baby?

5. The Israelites' hard bondage made their lives what?

Important Truths:

The Devil wants to destroy every believer.

We will have times of life that are hard.

God may bring trials into our lives even when we are doing right.

The Birth of Moses
Exodus 2:2-4
(Study: Exodus 2:1-10)

Hebrews 11:23 says, "By faith Moses, when he was born, was hid three months of his parents, because they saw he was a proper child; and they were not afraid of the king's commandment." Amram and Jochebed, Moses' parents, believed God had a purpose for their son and risked their own lives by keeping him alive. Pharaoh had ordered all the male Israelite babies to be killed by being thrown in the river. After hiding baby Moses in an ark of bulrushes, he was found by Pharaoh's daughter. She had compassion on the crying baby and took him as her own. She said she called him Moses, "because I drew him out of the water."

---

1. How long was Moses hid at home?

2. In what was Moses placed by the river?

3. Who watched over Moses in the ark?

4. Who found baby Moses?

5. Who were Moses' parents?

Important Truths:

God is preparing our future even as babies.

Parents have faith in what their children will be.

God uses unbelievers to invest in our lives.

Moses Murders
Exodus 2:11-13
(Study: Exodus 2:11-15)

Moses grew up in Pharaoh's household and was taught in all the wisdom of the Egyptians. When he was forty years old, it came into his heart to visit his brethren. Moses saw an Israelite suffer wrong by an Egyptian and he defended him and killed the Egyptian. The next day when he tried to solve an argument between two Israelites who were fighting, the one who did the wrong said, "Intendest thou to kill me, as thou killedst the Egyptian?" When Moses knew that it was known, he fled to a place called Midian. When Pharaoh heard of what had happened, he sought to kill Moses.

---

1. How old was Moses when he killed the Egyptian?

2. What was Moses taught?

3. What did Moses do with the man he killed?

4. Who wanted to kill Moses for murder?

5. To where did Moses flee?

Important Truths:

Murder is sin.

Our actions can be misunderstood.

Don't get into someone else's argument.

Moses at the Burning Bush
Exodus 3:3-5
(Study: Exodus 3:1-10)

Moses was leading his father-in-law's sheep on the backside of the desert on Mount Horeb. While there, Moses saw a bush burning that was not being consumed by the flame. He turned aside to see why the bush was not burnt, and the Lord called unto him out of the midst of the bush. Moses answered, "Here am I." God told Moses that He had seen the affliction that His people were going through in the land of Egypt, and that He would deliver them. God wanted Moses to confront Pharaoh and lead His people out of Egypt to go to the land of Canaan.

---

1. On what mountain was Moses?

2. What was Moses' answer when he was called?

3. Why did Moses need to take off his shoes?

4. What did God want Moses to do?

5. Whose affliction did God see?

Important Truths:

It was not the bush, but God in the bush!

Our response to God's call should be, "Here am I!"

Smaller jobs (leading sheep) prepare us for bigger jobs!

Moses' Excuses
Exodus 3:10-12
(Study: Exodus 3:1-4:20)

God told Moses at the burning bush to go to Pharaoh and tell him to let His people go. Moses began to make excuses why he could not do that. His first excuse was that they would not believe him (Exodus 4:1). His second excuse was that he was slow of speech and not eloquent (Exodus 4:10). God answered both of his excuses and promised to be with him and to send Aaron his brother as a spokesman for him. Moses answered God's call and returned to Jethro his father-in-law and told him that he must return to Egypt and see his brethren.

1. To whom did God send Moses?

2. Who was Moses' father-in-law?

3. What was Moses' first excuse?

4. What was Moses' second excuse?

5. Who did God send with Moses?

Important Truths:

Whom God calls, He qualifies.

God gives help to accomplish His will.

"I can do all things through Christ..."

Moses' Message Refused

Exodus 5:19-21
(Study: Exodus 5:1-23-6:1-13)

Moses obeyed God and went to the children of Israel in Egypt and let them know what God said and they believed. However, when Moses went and told Pharaoh that God said to let His people go, Pharaoh did not accept the message. In fact, he put more pressure upon the Israelites. The mistreatment by Pharaoh upon the Israelites caused them to doubt and murmur against Moses. Moses went back to the Lord and said, Pharaoh "hath done evil to this people; neither hast thou delivered thy people at all." Yet time would soon show differently.

---

1. Who did not accept God's message?

2. Who doubted God's message?

3. What were the Israelites required to make?

4. To whom did Moses go when his message was rejected?

5. What caused the Israelites to doubt?

Important Truths:

Opposition will often precede victory.

We must live by faith, not by sight.

Believers (Israelites) and unbelievers (Pharaoh) can discourage us from fulfilling God's will.

The Ten Plagues
Exodus 7:1-3
(Study: Exodus 7:1-16)

When Pharaoh refused to let the children of Israel go, God began to smite Egypt with plagues. Pharaoh continued to harden his heart and refused to let Israel go. God sent upon Egypt ten plagues: water turned to blood, frogs, lice, flies, murrain of cattle, boils, hail, locusts, darkness, and the death of the firstborn. God told Moses "Pharaoh shall not hearken unto you, that I may lay my hand upon Egypt, and bring forth mine armies, and my people the children of Israel, out of the land of Egypt by great judgments. And the Egyptians shall know that I am the LORD" (Exodus 7:4,5). After the death of the firstborn, finally, Pharaoh let Israel go.

---

1. God sent how many plagues?

2. What plague caused Pharaoh to let Israel go?

3. Why would Pharaoh not let Israel go?

4. What were some of the plagues God sent on Egypt?

5. The Lord made Moses a what unto Pharaoh?

Important Truths:

Every man is subject to God.

God can do anything.

One day all people will know God is Lord of all.

Pharaoh's Magicians
Exodus 8:17-19
(Study: Exodus 8:6-19)

The contest between Moses and Pharaoh was a battle between God and Satan, light and darkness, and good and bad. Pharaoh's magicians duplicated a rod turning into a snake (7:11), water turning to blood (7:22), and frogs coming up from the waters (8:7). Yet, when God sent lice, the magicians could not copy it and said, "This is the finger of God" (8:18, 19). Satan will always be a counterfeiter! II Corinthians 11:14 says, "And no marvel; for Satan himself is transformed into an angel of light." Satan has look alike bibles, preachers, and churches, but they are counterfeit. To deceive people, Satan tries to make duplicates of everything godly.

---

1. What could the magicians not duplicate?

2. What did the magicians tell Pharaoh?

3. Satan himself is transformed into what?

4. What became lice?

5. Satan will always be a what?

Important Truths:

Satan will always try to trick you.

Satan's counterfeits will be close to the real thing.

There are some things Satan cannot duplicate.

Israelites Were to Be Different
Exodus 11:5-7
(Study: Exodus 11:1-10)

God is about to send His tenth and final plague upon the Egyptians for Pharaoh's refusal to let the Israelites go. The tenth plague would be the death of the firstborn. Moses said to Pharaoh that at midnight all the firstborn of Egypt would die. Yet, God said the Israelite firstborn would not die that Pharaoh might "know how that the LORD doth put a difference between the Egyptians and Israel." Pharaoh's heart was hardened and he would not let the Israelites go, but after the death of the firstborn throughout the land of Egypt, he did. The children of Israel were God's chosen people and were different from the Egyptians.

---

1. All of the what would die?

2. When would they die?

3. God put a difference between what two different groups?

4. Why would Pharaoh not let Israel go?

5. Who are God's chosen people?

Important Truths:

Believers and unbelievers are different!

God has a way of changing people's minds.

Human life is in God's hand.

The Passover
Exodus 12:5-7
(Study: Exodus 12:1-20)

The last of the ten plagues was the death of the firstborn. God told Moses that in order to be spared from the death angel coming into an Israelite house, that they must kill a lamb and put the blood on the lintel and the two side posts. The lamb had to be a male and without blemish. At midnight, the death angel would come through and see the blood and pass over that house. Hence, the word "Passover" would be remembered for the night that God delivered Israel from bondage and the firstborn of Egypt died. The Passover would be an ordinance for Israel to keep for ever.

---

1. What was the tenth plague?

2. What would the death angel see to cause him to pass over?

3. The lamb had to be what?

4. Where did they put the blood?

5. How long was Israel to keep the Passover?

> **Important Truths:**
>
> The Passover Lamb was a picture of Jesus Christ.
>
> The Lord's Supper is the Christian's Passover.
>
> The blood was important!

Israel Leaves Egypt
Exodus 12:30-32
(Study: Exodus 12:21-51)

The tenth plague affected all the Egyptians. At midnight the death angel passed over Egypt and killed all the firstborn of man and beast. "There was not a house where there was not one dead." Only in Goshen, where the children of Israel lived, was there not anyone or anything killed because they put blood on the door post of their houses. When the death angel saw the blood, he would pass over the house. That night Pharaoh called for Moses and told him and all of Israel to go and leave the land of Egypt. God had the Israelites borrow from the Egyptians as they left Egypt and they gave the Israelites such things as they required.

---

1. Who did the tenth plague affect?

2. Were there any houses in Egypt where not one died?

3. How many in Goshen died?

4. What did the Israelites do before they left Egypt?

5. Who told Moses to "go, serve the LORD"?

Important Truths:

God can change your mind.

God does not want us to be in the world (Egypt).

The world (Egypt) does not like believers (Israelites).

Israel Crossing the Red Sea
Exodus 14:13-15
(Study: Exodus 14:1-31)

When the Israelites left Egypt they spoiled the Egyptians by borrowing jewels and raiment from them. Pharaoh's hard heart caused him to pursue Israel. The Lord led Israel to the Red Sea which caused them to be trapped between Pharaoh and the sea. The angel of God, in the form of a pillar of cloud, went between the camp of the Egyptians and the Israelites, so they could not come to one another. That night God parted the Red Sea, and the children of Israel crossed through it on dry ground. The Egyptians pursued Israel into the sea only to be destroyed. God took off their chariot wheels and then caused them to be drowned. "There remained not so much as one of them."

1. Who led Israel to the Red Sea?

2. Who stood between both armies?

3. When Israel crossed the Red Sea, the ground was what?

4. How many Egyptians died?

5. What did Moses tell Israel to do?

Important Truths:

God always has a plan and purpose.

The Lord will fight for us.

Go forward by faith!

Israel Murmurs
Exodus 15:24-26
(Study: Exodus 15:22-27)

The children of Israel saw God part the Red Sea and destroy Pharaoh and his army. Three days later, they got thirsty and murmured against Moses. Murmuring is complaining. They asked Moses, "What shall we drink?" The Lord told Moses to cast a certain tree into the waters, and the waters were made sweet. It was at the wilderness of Shur that the Lord proved and tested Israel. The Lord was not going to lead His people out of Egypt to die in the wilderness. God changed bitter water into sweet water for Israel. Instead of trusting the Lord, they murmured about how they perceived they were not taken care of by Moses and God.

---

1. What is murmuring?

2. How many days after the Red Sea did the children of Israel complain?

3. Against whom did they murmur?

4. Where did God prove and test Israel?

5. What did Moses put in the water?

Important Truths:

God hears us when we murmur.

We murmur because we forget God's goodness.

The tree (cross) made something sweet that was bitter.

Manna

Exodus 16:2-4
(Study: Exodus 16:1-36)

A month and a half after leaving Egypt, the children of Israel complained to Moses about not having anything to eat. Moses reminded them that "your murmurings are not against us, but against the LORD." God heard their murmurings and sent them manna. Manna "was like coriander seed, white; and the taste of it was like wafers made with honey." The Israelites were to gather it every morning according to their eating. On the sixth day, they were to gather twice as much, because on the seventh day (Sabbath Day) there would be none to gather. God gave the Israelites manna for 40 years until they came to Canaan.

1. What did Manna taste like?

2. How long would Israel eat manna?

3. Why would they not gather manna on the seventh day?

4. Who murmured against Moses and Aaron in the wilderness?

5. God rained what from Heaven for them?

Important Truths:

God provides for our physical needs.

Our complaining is against God not man.

We should honor the Lord's Day.

Aaron and Hur
Exodus 17:11-13
(Study: Exodus 17:8-16)

The Amalekites came to fight against Israel. Moses told Joshua to choose men and go out and fight against them. Moses went to the top of the hill that overlooked the battle and took the rod of God in his hand. "And it came to pass, when Moses held up his hand, that Israel prevailed: and when he let down his hand, Amalek prevailed" (Exodus 17:11). Moses' hands became heavy, so Aaron and Hur helped hold his hands up until the going down of the sun. Joshua and Israel won the battle that day and beat Amalek. God told Moses, "the LORD will have war with Amalek from generation to generation (Exodus 17:16). Amalek was the grandson of Esau and is a picture of the flesh.

---

1. Who helped Moses?

2. Who led Israel into battle?

3. Against whom did Israel fight?

4. Of what is Amalek a picture?

5. Who won the battle?

Important Truths:

There is a need for men to help God's man.

We will have to continually battle our flesh.

A war is not won with just one person.

The Ten Commandments

Exodus 20:18-20
(Study: Exodus 20:1-26)

Moses went up to Mount Sinai to meet with the Lord for the children of Israel. On two tables of stone, God used His finger to write ten commandments that we should learn, keep, and do. Those commandments, in order, are: Thou shalt have no other gods before Me; Thou shalt not make unto thee any graven images; Thou shalt not take the name of the Lord thy God in vain; Remember the Sabbath day to keep it holy; Honour thy father and mother; Thou shalt not kill; Thou shalt not commit adultery; Thou shalt not steal; Thou shalt not bear false witness; and Thou shalt not covet.

1. How many commandments were given?

2. What is the first commandment?

3. Where did Moses receive them?

4. What should we learn, keep, and do?

5. Fear of God would keep Israel from what?

Important Truths:

Each commandment has an important meaning.

God gives to the man of God what we need to hear.

All the law is fulfilled by loving God with all your heart, and loving your neighbor as yourself.

The Tabernacle
Exodus 25:8-10
(Study: Exodus 25:1-27:21)

God told Moses to build a tabernacle for the purpose of having a place that the presence of God would be among His people. This tabernacle would be a portable place of worship. The tabernacle was approximately 45 feet long and 15 feet wide. The court that went around the tabernacle was approximately 150 feet long and 75 feet wide. The tabernacle would be divided by a vail to separate the holy place from the Holy of Holies. The furniture in the Holy Place was: the candlestick, the table of showbread, and the altar of incense. In the Holy of Holies was the ark of the covenant. Years later, the tabernacle would be replaced by the temple when Israel was in the promised land and Solomon was king.

---

1. How big was the tabernacle?

2. How big was the court of the tabernacle?

3. Who gave Moses the pattern for building it?

4. Where was the ark of the covenant?

5. What replaced the tabernacle?

Important Truths:

We are the temple of the Holy Spirit.

We have direct access to God.

We should worship God.

Bezaleel

Exodus 31:1-3
(Study: Exodus 31:1-11)

God commanded Moses to build a tabernacle, and then provided the skilled workers to do it. God specifically called Bezaleel to build the tabernacle. God also gave someone to assist Bezaleel named Aholiab. God filled both of them "with wisdom of heart, to work all manner of work" (Exodus 35:35). The two of them would teach others to help in building this portable place of worship called the tabernacle (Exodus 35:34). Bezaleel was willing to be used of God to build and to teach others. God gave Bezaleel a call to serve, wisdom to do it, help to build, and the materials to complete it. All Bezaleel had to do was be willing, and he was!

---

1. Whom did God call by name?

2. With what five things did God fill Bezaleel?

3. Whom did God give to Bezaleel for help?

4. What was the portable place of worship?

5. Bezaleel did what he did because he was what?

Important Truths:

Whom God calls, He qualifies.

God gives help to those who need it.

We should be willing to teach others.

The Golden Calf
Exodus 32:2-4
(Study: Exodus 32:1-6)

The Lord called Moses up to the top of Mount Sinai to give him the pattern of the tabernacle and the Ten Commandments (Exodus 19:18-20). When the people thought Moses was gone too long, they came to Aaron and said, "Up, make us gods, which shall go before us." Aaron heeded their requests and took from them earrings of gold and made them a molten calf. The Israelites recognized this golden calf as the god that brought them out of Egypt instead of God Jehovah. The next day "the people sat down to eat and to drink, and rose up to play" (Exodus 32:6).

---

1. Who made the golden calf?

2. From what was the golden calf made?

3. Where was Moses?

4. Who said the golden calf was their god?

5. Aaron fashioned the golden calf with what?

Important Truths:

Trouble happens when there is an absence of godly leadership.

No man can serve two masters.

Leadership should not follow, but lead.

On the Lord's Side
Exodus 32:26-28
(Study: Exodus 32:1-35)

The children of Israel sinned a great sin by making the golden calf. When Moses came down from the mountain, "he took the calf which they had made, and burnt it in the fire, and ground it to powder, and strawed it upon the water, and made the children of Israel drink of it" (Exodus 32:20). He told the Israelites to consecrate themselves and when they did not, he asked for those to step forward who were on the Lord's side. The children of Levi stepped forward. Moses commanded them to execute judgement against those who disobeyed, and 3,000 men were slain.

---

1. Who said, "Who is on the LORD's side"?

2. What tribe chose to be on the Lord's side?

3. What did Moses do to the golden calf?

4. How many died for their disobedience?

5. Worshipping the golden calf was a great what?

Important Truths:

There are two sides, and we must choose which side we will be on.

The losing side is always those who oppose God.

The hardest stand to take is against sin that family chooses to do presumptuously.

Offering for the Tabernacle
Exodus 36:5-7
(Study: Exodus 36:1-7)

On Mt. Sinai, God gave Moses the pattern for the tabernacle. The materials for the tabernacle would come from the freewill offerings of the children of Israel. God told Moses that Bezaleel and Aholiab would lead in the making and building of the tabernacle. When Moses asked the people to give an offering for the building of the tabernacle, they gave willingly and abundantly. The people had given so much that they "were restrained from bringing."

1. Who was asked to give for building the tabernacle?

2. Did they give enough?

3. Whom did God have build the tabernacle?

4. The people had given so much that they were what?

5. How did the people give to the offering for the tabernacle?

Important Truths:

God wants willing and cheerful givers.

Money should be used for God's glory.

God's people have what is needed for God's work, but we must be willing to give it.

Strange Fire
Leviticus 10:1-3
(Study: Leviticus 10:1-7)

Nadab and Abihu were priests and sons of Aaron the high priest. When the tabernacle was set up, God sent fire down from Heaven to start the fire on the brazen altar (Leviticus 9:24). Nadab and Abihu started their own fire instead of using the fire that God gave. The word "strange" means foreign or to turn aside. God sent a fire down to devour Nadab and Abihu. Both of them were killed by God for using a fire "which he commanded them not."

1. What position did Nadab and Abihu hold?

2. Who was the father of Nadab and Abihu?

3. How did God kill Nadab and Abihu?

4. What did Nadab and Abihu offer before the Lord?

5. God said that before the people He would be what?

Important Truths:

God takes His commands seriously.

Leaders are more accountable to do God's work God's way.

Don't start your own fire.

The Man Who Blasphemed
Leviticus 24:10-12
(Study: Leviticus 24:10-23)

This unnamed young man blasphemed the name of the Lord and cursed. He was the son of an Israelitish woman and his father was an Egyptian. He got into an argument with a man in the camp and apparently lost his temper and let words come out of his mouth for which God held him accountable. God said for such actions, "he that blasphemeth the name of the LORD, he shall surely be put to death" (Leviticus 24:16). So the young man was taken outside the camp and stoned to death by the children of Israel. God said, "Whosoever curseth his God shall bear his sin," (Leviticus 24:15) and this young man did.

---

1. What sin did the young man commit?

2. What was his punishment?

3. Why did the young man curse?

4. What nationalities were his parents?

5. "Whosoever curseth his God shall" do what with his sin?

Important Truths:

Cursing is a sin.

God does not hold guiltless those who use His name in vain.

Sins of the father can visit the son.

The Guiding Cloud
Numbers 9:16-18
(Study: Numbers 9:15:23)

When the children of Israel came out of Egypt to go to the Promised Land, God led them with a pillar of cloud by day and a pillar of fire by night. God's presence was always with the children of Israel. When they were not traveling, the cloud would cover the tabernacle. "At the commandment of the LORD the children of Israel journeyed, and at the commandment of the LORD they pitched." The Israelites knew when and where to go by following the cloud. The cloud could tarry "two days, or a month, or a year," but the Israelites were only to move as the cloud did.

---

1. What appearance did the cloud have at night?

2. How often was the cloud with Israel?

3. Where was the cloud when Israel was not journeying?

4. What let Israel know when and where to go?

5. Where was the cloud leading them?

> **Important Truths:**
>
> The presence of the Lord is always with us.
>
> We need God's direction for everything.
>
> God's direction always has a destination.

The People Discourage Moses
Numbers 11:16-18
(Study: Numbers 11:1-30)

God had given the children of Israel manna to eat, but they were not satisfied. They complained that they had no meat to eat. Moses got discouraged with the people's murmuring and complaining and told God, "I am not able to bear all this people alone, because it is too heavy for me" (Numbers 11:14). God told Moses to gather 70 elders of the people and He would take the spirit that was upon him and put it upon them to help him bear the burden of the people. When the spirit of God rested upon the elders they prophesied and Moses said, "…would God that all the LORD'S people were prophets, and that the LORD would put his spirit upon them" (Numbers 11:29).

---

1. Was Moses able to bear the burden?

2. How many helped Moses with his burden?

3. What was Moses' burden?

4. What was discouraging to Moses?

5. About what did Israel complain?

Important Truths:

People can be a burden.

God gives us people to help us with burdens.

The Spirit of God can take care of any burden.

Miriam & Aaron Criticize
Numbers 12:1-3
(Study: Numbers 12:1-16)

Miriam and Aaron criticized their brother Moses for marrying an Ethiopian woman. God heard what they said, "and the anger of the LORD was kindled against them." God asked them, "Wherefore then were ye not afraid to speak against my servant Moses?" God struck Miriam with leprosy for her criticism. "Moses cried unto the LORD, saying, Heal her now, O God, I beseech thee." God said she should be ashamed for what she had done and she would be shut out of the camp for seven days. The children of Israel would not continue their journey until Miriam was brought in again.

---

1. How were Miriam and Aaron related to Moses?

2. What was Moses above all men?

3. For what did they criticize Moses?

4. What happened to Miriam because she was critical?

5. How long did Miriam have leprosy?

Important Truths:

God hears us when we criticize.

God punishes those who are critical.

We do not need to retaliate against those who criticize us.

The Twelve Spies
Numbers 13:28-30
(Study: Numbers 13:1-33)

When Israel got to the border of the Promised Land, they asked Moses to send men in to search out the land. Moses liked their idea and took twelve men, one of every tribe, to send into the land of Canaan (Deuteronomy 1:22, 23). Unfortunately, "they brought up an evil report of the land which they had searched." Only two of the spies, Joshua and Caleb, believed the Lord and encouraged the people to go in. The other ten, by their report, discouraged the people, and caused them to murmur against Moses, and rebel against the commandment of the Lord.

---

1. How many spies went into Canaan?

2. Who were the good spies?

3. The evil report caused Israel to murmur against whom?

4. Who said, "Let us go up at once, and possess it?"

5. Who said that the people of Canaan land were strong and the city walls were very great?

Important Truths:

Words can cause death or life.

Doing right can put you in the minority.

God is bigger than any giant.

Forfeiting the Promised Land

Numbers 14:29-31
(Study: Numbers 14:1-45)

The children of Israel were led out of Egypt after seeing God judge Egypt by the ten plagues. They crossed the Red Sea on dry ground and were fed with manna from Heaven. When they got to the border of Canaan, the Promised Land, they sent in spies to see the land, only to be discouraged from going in. Because of their unbelief, all those 20 and older would not be allowed to go in. Joshua and Caleb would be the only exception because they had faith and wholly followed the Lord. Those 19 and under would wander for 40 years in the wilderness while they waited for their unbelieving fathers to die before going into the promised land.

---

1. From what age and up would not go into Canaan?

2. Which two spies believed God?

3. How many years would Israel wander in the wilderness for not believing God?

4. What age did God consider the "little ones"?

5. Against whom did Israel murmur?

Important Truths:

God's promises can be forfeited by unbelief.

God rewards those who believe Him.

Children are affected by their parent's actions.

Korah and His Company
Numbers 16:1-3
(Study: Numbers 16:1-35)

Korah was a Levite who was separated from the congregation of Israel to do the service of the tabernacle of the Lord. Korah, Dathan, and Abiram took with them 250 princes of Israel and gathered themselves against Moses and Aaron. They accused Moses of taking too much upon himself and lifting himself above the congregation. Moses assured them that the Lord had sent him and that God had done all the works since leaving Egypt. Because of their murmurings and false accusations, God had the earth open up and swallow Korah, Dathan, and Abiram with all their houses. Then God sent fire from Heaven and killed the 250 princes.

1. Korah was from what tribe?

2. How many princes followed Korah?

3. Who was accused of taking too much upon himself?

4. What happened to Korah, Dathan, and Abiram for their murmuring?

5. How did the princes die that followed Korah?

Important Truths:

Do not speak against the man of God.

Be satisfied with the ministry God has given you.

Be careful whom you follow.

Aaron's Rod that Budded

Numbers 17:3-5
(Study: Numbers 17:1-13)

Even after the earth swallowed up Korah and fire killed the 250 princes who caused rebellion, the Israelites told Moses, "Ye have killed the people of the LORD" (16:41). God told Moses, "I will make to cease from me the murmurings of the children of Israel, whereby they murmur against you." Moses collected one rod from each of the tribes of Israel and put their names on it. For the tribe of Levi he put Aaron's name. He put the rods in the tabernacle before the Lord. The next morning Aaron's rod budded, bloomed blossoms, and yielded almonds. The rod would be kept as a token against the rebels, and to silence their murmurings.

---

1. Who did Israel say killed Korah?

2. Whose name went on the rod for Levi?

3. Where were the rods put overnight?

4. What happened to Aaron's rod?

5. Aaron's rod that budded would be kept as a token against whom?

Important Truths:

God does not like murmuring!

God can take something dead and make it alive.

People can be blinded to the truth.

Moses Strikes the Rock

Numbers 20:11-13
(Study: Numbers 20:2-13)

The children of Israel complained to Moses about not having water. Moses took their complaint to the Lord. God told Moses to "Take the rod, and gather thou the assembly together, thou, and Aaron thy brother, and speak ye unto the rock before their eyes; and it shall give forth his water" (v.8). Instead of speaking to the rock, Moses "smote the rock twice and water came out abundantly" (v.11). The Lord told Moses and Aaron, "Because ye believed me not, to sanctify me in the eyes of the children of Israel, therefore ye shall not bring this congregation into the land which I have given them."

---

1. About what did Israel complain?

2. What was Moses to do to the rock?

3. What did Moses do to the rock?

4. What did Moses' disobedience cost him?

5. What was the water called?

> **Important Truths:**
>
> We should do things the way God says.
>
> God holds leadership more accountable.
>
> Christians should act and not react to people.

Fiery Serpents
Numbers 21:5-7
(Study: Numbers 21:2-9)

The children of Israel were discouraged because of their difficulties and began to speak against God and Moses for bringing them up out of Egypt. God sent fiery serpents among the people and many died. Israel confessed they had sinned and asked Moses to pray for God to take away the serpents. God told Moses, "Make thee a fiery serpent, and set it upon a pole: and it shall come to pass, that every one that is bitten, when he looketh upon it, shall live." Those who would choose to look at the brazen serpent would live from the snake bite, but if they did not they would die.

---

1. Why did Israel complain?

2. What did God send to bite the people?

3. What did Moses make to save the lives of those bitten?

4. What did a person do to be healed?

5. Who prayed for the people?

Important Truths:

Discouragement can make you do dumb things.

Salvation is a choice.

Sin has consequences.

Balaam's Donkey Talks

Numbers 22:28-30
(Study: Numbers 22:1-35)

Balak the king of Moab wanted to curse the children of Israel so he could defeat them in battle. He called for a soothsayer named Balaam to curse the children of Israel. At first, Balaam would not come to King Balak, because God told him not to go. King Balak sent again to ask Balaam to come and curse Israel, and he went because God gave him permission to go. God was angry with Balaam for going, and placed an angel in his way as an adversary against him. Three times Balaam's donkey kept the angel from killing Balaam. Balaam, not seeing the angel, smote his donkey for not going in the path. God opened the mouth of the donkey and the eyes of Balaam, to see the angel and his error.

---

1. Where was Balak king?

2. Whom did Balak want Balaam to curse?

3. What was Balaam?

4. What was standing in the way to kill Balaam?

5. How many times did the donkey save Balaam's life?

Important Truths:

There is a difference between God's perfect will and permissive will.

You should never wish evil against Israel.

God can even use a donkey.

Balaam Blesses Israel

Numbers 24:8-10
(Study: Numbers 24:1-25)

Balak, king of Moab, offered to give Balaam money and promotion if he would curse the children of Israel. God would not allow Balaam to do so because they were His chosen people. Many years before, God had promised Abraham, "And I will bless them that bless thee, and curse him that curseth thee: and in thee shall all families of the earth be blessed" (Genesis 12:3). Three times King Balak tried to get Balaam to curse Israel and he could not. God told Balaam that "He hath not beheld iniquity in Jacob, neither hath he seen perverseness in Israel: the LORD his God is with him, and the shout of a king is among them" (Numbers 23:21).

---

1. To whom did God first promise His blessings on Israel?

2. How many times did Balak try to curse Israel?

3. Why was Balak angry with Balaam?

4. What would Balak give Balaam for cursing Israel?

5. What will you get for blessing Israel?

Important Truths:

God loves the children of Israel.

God blesses those who bless Israel.

God curses those who curse Israel.

The Counsel of Balaam

Numbers 25:1-3
(Study: Numbers 25:1-9)

Balaam missed out on the rewards of his divination for not cursing Israel for King Balak. So Balaam "taught Balac to cast a stumblingblock before the children of Israel, to eat things sacrificed unto idols, and to commit fornication" (Revelation 2:14). Balaam knew he could not curse Israel, but he knew if the Israelites sinned against God that He would chastise them. God killed 24,000 Israelites for going and sinning with the Moabites. Moses reminded Israel after defeating the Moabites, "Behold, these caused the children of Israel, through the counsel of Balaam, to commit trespass against the LORD in the matter of Peor, and there was a plague among the congregation of the LORD" (Numbers 31:16).

---

1. What did Balaam teach Balak?

2. How many Israelites died for their sin?

3. What was Israel's sin?

4. The anger of the Lord was kindled against whom?

5. Balaam counseled how to destroy Israel so that he could receive what?

> **Important Truths:**
>
> Walk not in the counsel of the ungodly.
>
> God does not take sin lightly.
>
> The devil wants you under God's chastening hand.

The Zeal of Phinehas

Numbers 25:11-13
(Study: Numbers 25:1-18)

Through the counsel of Balaam, the Israelites committed fornication and bowed down to the Moabite idols. Moses told the people to slay every one that was joined unto Baal-peor. One of the Israelites, in his rebellion, "brought unto his brethren a Midianitish woman in the sight of Moses, and in the sight of all the congregation of the children of Israel." However, Phinehas "rose up from among the congregation, and took a javelin in his hand; And he went after the man of Israel into the tent, and thrust both of them through….So the plague was stayed from the children of Israel." God honored the zeal of Phinehas and promised him peace and an everlasting priesthood because he made an atonement for Israel.

---

1. Whose counsel caused Israel to sin?

2. What was Israel's sin?

3. What did an Israelite bring before the congregation?

4. What did Phinehas do to the rebels?

5. Phinehas made what for Israel?

> **Important Truths:**
>
> One man can make a difference.
>
> Zeal should be for God.
>
> God rewards what we do for Him.

Moses' Replacement
Numbers 27:16-18
(Study: Numbers 27:12-23)

God told Moses he could see the Promised Land, but he would not be allowed to go into it, because of his disobedience. When the people were in need of water, Moses hit the rock instead of speaking to it like God told him. Moses asked God who was to lead in his place. God answered him that Joshua would be his replacement. God told Moses to lay his hand upon Joshua, give him a charge and "put some of thine honour upon him, that all the congregation of the children of Israel may be obedient." Moses brought Joshua before all the congregation and did as the Lord commanded him. Joshua would become the next leader of Israel.

---

1. Who chose Joshua as the next leader?

2. Moses did not want the Israelites to be like what?

3. What did God say was in Joshua?

4. What would Moses put upon Joshua that would cause the Israelites to be obedient?

5. Why could Moses not go into Canaan?

Important Truths:

One sin can cause you to miss out.

God chooses who the leader is.

Servants become leaders.

Borderline Tribes

Numbers 32:4-6
(Study: Numbers 32:1-42)

Israel left Egypt and got to the border of the Promised Land. The tribes of Gad and Rueben came to Moses and asked to stay on this side Jordan and have it for their inheritance. Moses first resisted because they would discourage the rest of the tribes by not going in and helping possess the land. Rueben and Gad promised to go over Jordan armed to help the brethren "until the children of Israel have inherited every man his inheritance." Moses said the tribe of Rueben, Gad, and the half tribe of Manasseh could have their request as long as they went in with the rest of Israel to take possession of the land.

---

1. Who asked to dwell outside of Canaan?

2. Why did they ask this?

3. What did Moses say they would do to the rest of the tribes for not going in and helping possess the land?

4. What did they promise to do?

5. Which tribes took their inheritance on the other side of Jordan?

Important Truths:

Sometimes we choose good instead of best.

Our actions can discourage others.

It is better to not be on the borderline of God's will.

Reminding the Next Generation
Deuteronomy 1:1-3
(Study: Deuteronomy 1-3)

The word "Deuteronomy" means second law. The Israelites age twenty and up would perish for their unbelief when they searched out Canaan. For forty years, they wandered in the wilderness and died, except for Joshua and Caleb, because they wholly followed the Lord. Moses spoke to this new generation and reviewed all that God had done for them since they left the land of Egypt. Moses reminded them of the wars in which God gave them victory, the judges that helped Him keep order, the ten spies that discouraged the people, the battles on this side of Jordan, and their new leader, Joshua, whom they would follow.

---

1. How many days journey were they from Kadesh-barnea when at Mount Seir?

2. How many years would Israel wander in the wilderness for their unbelief?

3. What does "Deuteronomy" mean?

4. Who wholly followed the Lord?

5. Who would lead Israel after Moses?

Important Truths:

Teach the next generation all that God has done.

There are things to learn from previous generations.

Learn from history, or repeat its mistakes.

Moses' Last Counsels

Deuteronomy 31:1-3
(Study: Deuteronomy 31:1-30)

Moses was not able to go into the Promised Land because of disobeying God at the waters of Meribah. Moses was about to die and he called Israel together to give them his last counsels. He told them to "Be strong and of a good courage, fear not, nor be afraid of them: for the LORD thy God, he it is that doth go with thee; he will not fail thee, nor forsake thee." Then Moses told Joshua, "Be strong and of a good courage: for thou must go with this people unto the land which the LORD hath sworn unto their fathers to give them; and thou shalt cause them to inherit it." The last thing he gave them was the written law and he told them to continually read it and hear it.

---

1. What kept Moses from Canaan land?

2. Who would not fail or forsake Israel?

3. How old was Moses when he gave his counsel?

4. Who would take Moses' place?

5. What was Israel to read and hear?

Important Truths:

Listen to godly counsel.

Follow godly leadership.

Read and hear the Word of God.

The Song of Moses

Deuteronomy 31:28-30
(Study: Deuteronomy 32:1-44)

Moses was about to die and told Israel, "…ye have been rebellious against the LORD; and how much more after my death?" Moses gave them two things as reminders to do right. One was the book of the law and the other was a song. In the song Moses reminded them how good God is and what He has done for them. Then Moses spoke prophetically and revealed that their fullness would lead to their forgetfulness of God and His goodness. He also told them that their sin would bring God's judgement. The end of the song reminds Israel of God's healing and mercy if they returned to Him.

1. What would Israel do in the sight of the Lord?

2. What two things did Moses give Israel as reminders?

3. Moses' song reminded Israel that God is what?

4. Of what two things did the end of the song remind Israel?

5. Israel's fullness allowed for what?

Important Truths:

Fullness allows for forgetfulness of God's goodness.

Even knowing our future actions, God is good to us.

Music can be a good teacher.

The Death of Moses

Deuteronomy 34:4-6
(Study: Deuteronomy 34:1-12)

Moses was a great leader and servant of the Lord. God used him to bring the children of Israel out of Egypt and lead them to the border of Canaan Land. Joshua would be the next leader and would take the Israelites into the Promised Land. Because Moses disobeyed the Lord he was not able to go into Canaan. God did allow him to see the land but not go into it. Before Moses died, God took him to the top of Mount Pisgah to shew him the land of Israel. "Moses was an hundred and twenty years old when he died: his eye was not dim, nor his natural force abated."

1. Who followed Moses as leader of Israel?

2. How old was Moses when he died?

3. From where did Moses get to see the Promised Land?

4. Why was Moses not allowed to go into the Promised Land?

5. Where was Moses buried?

Important Truths:

There are consequences to our sin.

You can either see or experience God's blessings.

God is in control of when you will die.

God Commissions Joshua
Joshua 1:1-3
(Study: Joshua 1:1-18)

After Moses died, Joshua became the new leader of Israel. God told Joshua that "as I was with Moses, so I will be with thee: I will not fail thee, nor forsake thee." Three times God told Joshua to be strong and courageous. He tells Joshua that his courage will come from the promise that God would be with him and he would have the book of the law to meditate upon. God told Joshua that if he would meditate and do His law, that he would prosper and have good success as the new leader of Israel.

1. What did God tell Joshua three times?

2. What did God promise Joshua He would not do?

3. Joshua was Moses' what?

4. Joshua was to meditate upon what?

5. What would happen to Joshua if he did God's law?

Important Truths:

Courage comes from God and His Word.

Obedience to God's Word is the recipe for success.

God commissions His leaders.

Rahab Hides the Spies
Joshua 2:9-11
(Study: Joshua 2:1-24)

Joshua prepares to go in and possess the Promised Land. Joshua sends two spies in to view the land, even Jericho. The spies are seen entering a harlot's house named Rahab. The king of Jericho sends soldiers to her house to apprehend the spies, but she tells them that they have already left and to pursue them quickly. Rahab hid the spies on the roof of her house among the stalks of flax. Hebrews 11:31 says, "By faith the harlot Rahab perished not with them that believed not, when she had received the spies with peace." Because she believed in God, she and her house were delivered from the destruction of Jericho. The spies told her to put a scarlet line in her window for her protection when they returned.

1. What occupation was Rahab?

2. How many spies did Joshua send into Jericho?

3. Where did Rahab hide the spies?

4. What was Rahab to put in her window?

5. Rahab perished not because of her what?

Important Truths:

Anyone can be saved if he will believe.

Her one decision to do right, saved her family.

God uses women who have faith.

Israel Crosses the Jordan River
Joshua 3:15-17
(Study: Joshua 3:1-17)

Israel has wandered in the wilderness for 40 years and is now ready to go into the Promised Land. Crossing the Jordan River would put them in Canaan. Joshua told the people to follow the Ark of the Covenant as they crossed over Jordan. The priests that bare the ark came to the Jordan River and as they touched the brim of the water, God parted the Jordan River. "And the priests that bare the ark of the covenant of the LORD stood firm on dry ground in the midst of Jordan, and all the Israelites passed over on dry ground, until all the people were passed clean over Jordan."

---

1. What did Israel follow?

2. Who went into the Jordan River first?

3. "The people passed over right against" where?

4. How was the ground described that Israel passed over?

5. Crossing the Jordan River would put the Israelites where?

Important Truths:

God does the impossible.

You must put your feet in the water for great things to happen.

Following God means you are going the right direction.

A Memorial for Israel
Joshua 4:5-7
(Study: Joshua 4:1-24)

The children of Israel crossed over the Jordan River on dry ground because God parted the water. God told Joshua to have one man from every tribe get a stone from the Jordan River and bring it out. Joshua took those twelve stones and made a memorial for Israel. Joshua told them that their children would ask in time to come, "What mean ye by these stones?" And that they would say, "Israel came over this Jordan on dry land." The purpose would be, "that all the people of the earth might know the hand of the LORD, that it is mighty: that ye might fear the LORD your God forever."

---

1. How many stones were used for the memorial?

2. What would children ask their fathers in time to come?

3. What river did Israel cross on dry ground?

4. The hand of the Lord is what?

5. How long was Israel to fear the Lord?

Important Truths:

Memorials keep important things in memory.

Have an answer when children ask, "Why?"

God's hand is mighty.

The Walls of Jericho
Joshua 6:20-22
(Study: Joshua 6:1-27)

After the children of Israel crossed the Jordan River, the first city they came to was Jericho. It was a walled city and nobody came in or out for fear of the Israelites. God told Joshua to have the children of Israel to follow the Ark of the Covenant, to march around the walls of Jericho once per day for six days, and to not say a word. On the seventh day, they were told to march around the wall seven times and then to shout. They did this and the walls of Jericho fell down flat, and they went in and utterly destroyed all that was in the city. Joshua spared the lives of Rahab and her family for hiding the spies.

---

1. Who in Jericho was spared?

2. On the seventh day, how many times did they march around Jericho?

3. How many was Israel to utterly destroy?

4. What fell down flat?

5. What did Israel follow around the walls of Jericho?

Important Truths:

God can break down any wall.

Obey God even when you do not understand.

God rewards those who help His people.

The Sin of Achan

Joshua 7:19-21
(Study: Joshua 7:1-26)

After the great victory at Jericho, there was great defeat at the next city called Ai. The Israelites were defeated and 36 men were killed. The reason for their loss was because Achan had stolen a Babylonish garment, 200 shekels of silver, and a wedge of gold at the conquest of Jericho. God said all of Israel would be accursed until they destroyed the accursed from among them. Joshua confronted Achan about his sin and he confessed to it all. Joshua said to Achan, "Why hast thou troubled us? the LORD shall trouble thee this day. And all Israel stoned him with stones, and burned them with fire, after they had stoned them with stones."

1. How many Israelites were killed at Ai?

2. What did Achan steal?

3. What happened to Achan because he stole?

4. Achan sinned against whom?

5. What caused Achan to steal?

Important Truths:

Our sin never affects just us.

God hates stealing.

Covetousness will ruin you.

League with Gibeonites
Joshua 9:12-14
(Study: Joshua 9:1-27)

After the children of Israel had destroyed the cities of Jericho and Ai, the people of the land became afraid. The inhabitants of Gibeon sent ambassadors to the children of Israel who were wearing old shoes and carrying moldy bread, hoping to trick them into making a league with them. The children of Israel made peace with the Gibeonites, without asking counsel of the Lord. Three days later they found out that the Gibeonites were their neighbors. Because of their promise, they could not destroy the Gibeonites and they made the Gibeonites their servants instead.

---

1. Who tricked the Israelites into making a league with them?

2. What did they use to trick them?

3. What should Israel have asked from the Lord?

4. Did Israel keep their promise to the Gibeonites?

5. What two cities did the Israelites destroy that caused the people of the land to be fearful?

Important Truths:

Always get counsel from God.

Realize that things are not always as they appear.

Keep your promises.

The Sun Stood Still
Joshua 10:12-14
(Study: Joshua 10:1-43)

Five kings of the Amorites gathered their armies together against Israel to go to battle. God fought for Israel that day and "cast down great stones from heaven upon them unto Azekah, and they died: they were more which died with hailstones than they whom the children of Israel slew with the sword." Joshua asked God to have the sun stand still so they could avenge themselves of their enemies. The sun stood still for about a whole day while the Israelites defeated their enemies. There has never been a day like that before or after it when God stopped the sun and moon.

---

1. How many kings fought against Israel?

2. How long did the sun stand still?

3. Who asked God to stop the sun?

4. More people died by what than with the sword?

5. Who fought for Israel?

Important Truths:

God fights for His own.

We can ask God to do the impossible.

God can allow us to accomplish more in a day than we think is possible.

Caleb's Mountain
Joshua 14:10-12
(Study: Joshua 14:1-15)

Joshua, the leader of Israel, began dividing up the land of Canaan to each tribe. Caleb came to him and reminded him of Moses' promise to the two of them. Moses said, "Surely the land whereon thy feet have trodden shall be thine inheritance, and thy children's for ever, because thou hast wholly followed the LORD my God." Caleb was 40 years old when he went in to spy out the land and came back with a good report. He is now 85 and tells Joshua "give me this mountain." Joshua blesses Caleb and gives him the mountain and the land of Hebron for an inheritance.

---

1. How old was Caleb when he spied out Canaan?

2. How old was Caleb when he asked for his mountain?

3. Which piece of land was Caleb's inheritance?

4. Why was Caleb given the mountain?

5. Who lived on Caleb's mountain?

Important Truths:

God rewards those who wholly follow Him.

You never get too old to go after a mountain.

God keeps His promises!

Cities of Refuge
Joshua 20:2-4
(Study: Joshua 20:1-9)

God told Moses and Joshua to make sure that there were places called "cities of refuge" throughout the land of Israel. The cities would be places of safety that a person, who had harmed another person by accident, could go. Once there, they would declare to the elders of the city what they had done and wait for judgement. If declared innocent, they would stay and live there until the death of the high priest, before returning home. The purpose would be to protect the innocent from being killed by an avenger of blood. God appointed six cities to be cities of refuge.

1. How many cities of refuge were there?

2. Who would a city of refuge keep safe?

3. These cities were a refuge from whom?

4. When could the innocent return home?

5. Who was protected in the city of refuge?

Important Truths:

Cities of refuge were a picture of salvation.

A third party can give unbiased judgement.

A person is innocent until proven guilty.

Joshua's Last Counsel
Joshua 23:6-8
(Study: Joshua 23:1-16)

Joshua is now old and realizes his time on earth is short. He calls all Israel together so he can give his final counsel and instruction. He reminds them how God has fought for them and "that not one thing hath failed of all the good things which the LORD" spake concerning them. Joshua charges them to obey, cleave to, and love the Lord their God. He warns them that if they do not obey God's law and they serve other gods, that "then shall the anger of the LORD be kindled against you, and ye shall perish quickly from off the good land which he hath given unto you."

---

1. What was one of the three things that Joshua charged the Israelites to do?

2. What were the Israelites to keep and do?

3. Israel was not to make mention of what?

4. To what was Israel to cleave?

5. What would happen if Israel served other gods?

Important Truths:

We should listen to the counsel of wise, old men.

Love and obedience go hand in hand.

Not one of God's promises will ever fail.

The Stone of Witness
Joshua 24:25-27
(Study: Joshua 24:1-33)

At the very end of his life, Joshua calls all Israel together and reminds them how their fathers served false gods. He tells them how good God was to deliver them from Egyptian bondage and to bring them to the land of Canaan. Joshua charges the children of Israel to "fear the LORD and serve him in sincerity and in truth." He gives personal testimony and tells them, "as for me and my house, we will serve the LORD." The people said "we will serve the LORD." Joshua set up a great stone by the sanctuary as a reminder to the children of Israel of their commitment to serve the Lord.

1. Who said, "as for me and my house, we will serve the LORD?"

2. Who also committed to serve the Lord?

3. The stone was a witness to their what?

4. Where was the stone placed?

5. What did Joshua charge the children of Israel to do?

Important Truths:

We should be committed to serve God.

Make physical reminders of spiritual decisions.

One man influenced others to serve God.

Another Generation
Judges 2:10-12
(Study: Judges 2:1-15)

When Israel went into the land of Canaan, they did not utterly drive out the inhabitants of the land and they began following their ways. "The people served the LORD all the days of Joshua, and all the days of the elders who outlived Joshua, and had seen all the great works of the LORD, that he did for Israel." Yet, "there arose another generation after them, which knew not the LORD, nor yet the works which he had done for Israel. And the children of Israel did evil in the sight of the LORD, and served Baalim." Because of Israel's sin, the anger and hand of the Lord was against them, and they were greatly distressed.

---

1. What did the new generation not know?

2. Who did Israel serve instead of God?

3. What did Israel follow of the people that were round about them?

4. What was against Israel?

5. Because of Israel's sin they were greatly what?

Important Truths:

Place yourself under good leadership.

Teach the next generation.

God will have no other gods before Him.

God Raises Up Judges
Judges 2:16-18
(Study: Judges 2:1-23)

God chose Moses to lead the children of Israel out of Egypt, and Joshua to lead them into the Promised Land. Once in the Promised Land, they had no leader. It was not long before the Israelites started serving false gods, which brought on them the anger and punishment of the Lord. The cycle of apostasy that Israel repeated seven times in the book of Judges was: they sinned against God, they were punished by God, they cried to God, and God delivered them. The judges were deliverers set up by God to lead Israel. Unfortunately, when the judge was dead, Israel would return to serving false gods and corrupt themselves more than their fathers.

1. What two people led Israel first?

2. What was a judge?

3. What was Israel's cycle of apostasy?

4. When would Israel return to false gods and corrupt themselves?

5. Who was with the judge?

Important Truths:

A good, God-sent leader is important.

Israel's cycle of apostasy was: they sinned, were punished, cried, and were delivered.

When there is no leader, be a leader.

Lefty Stabs Fatty
Judges 3:20-22
(Study: Judges 3:15-30)

The children of Israel did evil in the sight of the Lord and God strengthened Eglon, the king of Moab, against Israel. Israel served Moab 18 years. When the Israelites cried unto the Lord, He raised up a judge named Ehud. Ehud came to the king of Moab with a present and then told him he had a secret errand unto him. The king spoke with him alone, and Ehud with his left hand pulled a dagger and stabbed King Eglon in the belly. Eglon was so fat that the entire knife went into him and could not be retrieved. Ehud rallied the Israelites and they killed 10,000 Moabite soldiers. That day, Israel was freed from Moab and had rest for 80 years.

---

1. What was the name of the king of Moab?

2. What was the name of the judge?

3. What was unique about Ehud?

4. How many Moabite men were killed?

5. How long did Israel have rest?

Important Truths:

God can strengthen the enemy or you based on what you do.

A gift can blind the eyes.

One can make a difference.

A Tent Spike
Judges 4:19-21
(Study: Judges 4:1-24)

After Judge Ehud was dead, the Israelites did evil in the sight of the Lord. God put Israel under the hand of Jabin king of Canaan who mightily oppressed them for 20 years. The children of Israel cried unto the Lord for help and He sent them Deborah and Barak. Sisera, captain of Jabin's army went up against Israel and his entire army was killed. Sisera fled away on foot and hid in a tent where there was a woman named Jael, who was a Kenite. Sisera was so exhausted from the battle and running that he lay down in the tent to rest. While he slept, Jael took a hammer and tent spike and nailed Sisera's head to the ground and he died. Israel's enemy that day was killed by a woman who fought for Israel.

1. How many years was Israel oppressed?

2. What was the name of the Canaanite king?

3. Who led Israel's army?

4. Who was the captain of the Canaanite army?

5. Who killed Sisera?

Important Truths:

God uses women consecrated to Him.

One plus God makes the majority.

Use what you have for God's service.

Gideon's Fleece
Judges 6:36-38
(Study: Judges 6:1-40)

The Israelites did evil again in the sight of the Lord and He delivered them into the hand of Midian for seven years. "Israel was greatly impoverished because of the Midianites" and cried unto the Lord for help. God told Gideon, "Surely I will be with thee, and thou shalt smite the Midianites as one man." Gideon wanted a sign to know for sure that the Lord wanted him to lead Israel. Gideon told the Lord, "I will put a fleece of wool in the floor; and if the dew be on the fleece only, and it be dry upon all the earth beside, then shall I know that thou wilt save Israel by mine hand, as thou hast said." The Lord did as he asked, and then did the opposite and made the fleece dry and the ground wet with dew.

---

1. How long was Israel under the Midianites?

2. Who did God call to deliver Israel?

3. What did Gideon use to prove God?

4. How much dew was wrung out of the fleece?

5. Who said to Gideon, "I will be with thee?"

Important Truths:

You do not need signs to take God at His Word.

God can do anything!

God uses ordinary people for His purpose.

Gideon's 300 Men
Judges 7:6-8
(Study: Judges 7:1-15)

Gideon was a judge called of God to deliver Israel from the Midianites. The army of Midian totaled 135,000 and Gideon's army 300. When Gideon called Israel together to fight the Midianites, 32,000 men showed up. Yet, God said it was too many because Israel would vaunt themselves and say, "Mine own hand hath saved me." God told Gideon to allow the fearful and afraid to leave, so 22,000 went home. God said it was still too many and that He would put the rest to a test of how they drank water. Of the 10,000 that were left, only 300 passed the test and would go to fight the Midianites. God assured Gideon that these 300 were enough when Gideon heard the Midianites talk of a dream of their defeat.

---

1. How many Midianites were there?

2. How many men did Gideon have at the beginning?

3. How many went home fearful and afraid?

4. How many did not pass the drinking test?

5. How many went with Gideon to battle?

Important Truths:

The size of the enemy does not matter, only the level of your faith.

God will put us to the test.

Confidence is the assurance I am doing God's will.

Sword of the Lord & of Gideon

Judges 7:20-22
(Study: Judges 7:16-25)

Gideon divided his 300 men into three groups of one hundred and gave them a trumpet, and pitchers with lamps within them and placed them outside the camp of the Midianites. He told them that when he gave the signal, they were to blow their trumpets, break their pitchers, hold their lamps up and cry, "The sword of the LORD and of Gideon." They did this in the middle of the night "and the Lord set every man's sword against his fellow." The Midianites awoke out of sleep and began killing each other out of surprise and fear. Some 120,000 Midianites died in that first battle and 15,000 fled.

---

1. What did the Israelites cry in battle?

2. How many Midianites died?

3. How many fled away?

4. Gideon's army "stood every man in his" what?

5. Who caused the Midianites to kill each other?

Important Truths:

Much was accomplished with few, because they followed orders.

God's plans will not always seem logical.

Every person has a place.

Faint, Yet Pursuing
Judges 8:4-6
(Study: Judges 8:1-32)

God delivered the Midianites into Gideon's hand. The Midianites killed each other when Gideon and his 300 men blew their trumpets and shouted, "The sword of the Lord and of Gideon." Gideon and his men pursued after the remaining 15,000 Midianites and their two kings, Zebah and Zalmunna. Gideon's men were faint from the battle and stopped to ask for bread at two cities named Succoth and Penuel. Both cities refused to give Gideon and his men bread to eat. Gideon pursued anyway, smote the rest of the host of the Midianites, and killed their two kings. Upon returning, he punished the two cities that refused to give bread to him and his faint 300 men.

1. How many men were with Gideon?

2. How many Midianites fled away?

3. Which two kings did Gideon pursue?

4. Who refused to give Gideon bread?

5. Gideon and his men were faint, yet they still did what?

Important Truths:

Keep going even when you are faint.

Help those who are weary and tired.

Finish the job God has called you to do.

Conspiracy of Abimelech
Judges 9:3-5
(Study: Judges 9:1-57)

As soon as Gideon was dead, the children of Israel returned to following idols. One of the sons of Gideon was named Abimelech, who was born of a concubine. After his father's death, Abimelech gathered men from Shechem to make himself king. To secure this position, he went to his father's house and killed 70 of his brothers. Jotham, the youngest, escaped being murdered by his brother. Jotham told the men of Shechem and his brother Abimelech that because of their treachery, the two of them would devour one another. After three years, Jotham's curse came to pass and the men of Shechem and Abimelech were killed.

---

1. How many sons did Gideon have?

2. Who killed his brothers to be king?

3. How many brothers did he kill?

4. Who was the youngest son of Gideon?

5. How many years did Abimelech reign?

> **Important Truths:**
>
> God does not allow wickedness to go unpunished.
>
> Covetousness will destroy family relationships.
>
> Bad things happen to good people.

Jephthah's Vow
Judges 11:30-32
(Study: Judges 11:1-40)

Jephthah was cast out of his house by his brethren because he was the son of a strange woman. In the process of time, the Ammonites made war with Israel and Jephthah was called back home to lead Israel in battle. Jephthah made a vow that if God would deliver the Ammonites into his hands "that whatsoever cometh forth of the doors of my house to meet me, when I return in peace from the children of Ammon, shall surely be the LORD'S, and I will offer it up for a burnt offering." The children of Ammon were defeated and when Jephthah returned home the first thing out of his house was his only daughter. Jephthah "did with her according to his vow which he had vowed."

---

1. Who cast Jephthah out of his house?

2. Who fought against Israel?

3. What did Jephthah vow?

4. Who delivered the Ammonites to Jephthah?

5. Who did Jephthah sacrifice for a victory?

Important Truths:

Be careful what you vow to the Lord.

Always keep your vows to the Lord.

God takes seriously what we vow.

Jealousy of Ephraim
Judges 12:1-3
(Study: Judges 12:1-7)

After Jephthah defeated the Ammonites, the children of Ephraim came to Jephthah and threatened to burn him and his house for not calling them to go to battle with him. Instead of rejoicing in the victory that God gave Jephthah over the Ammonites, they complained that they were not invited to come fight. Jephthah did not take kindly to their threats and gathered the men of Gilead to fight the men of Ephraim. Jephthah won in battle and "there fell at that time of the Ephraimites forty and two thousand." For six years, Jephthah would judge Israel.

1. Why were the Ephramites upset?

2. What did they threaten to do?

3. How many Ephraimites died?

4. How long was Jephthah judge?

5. Who did Jephthah say delivered the Ammonites into his hand?

Important Truths:

Jealousy will get you into trouble.

Rejoice in other people's blessings.

Jealousy can hurt a lot of innocent people.

Birth of Samson
Judges 13:3-5
(Study: Judges 13:1-25)

The children of Israel did evil again and were under the hand of the Philistines for 40 years. God sent an angel to Manoah and his wife to tell them that they would have a son who would be a Nazarite. A Nazarite was one who was consecrated to God. The boy to be born would be called Samson and he would judge Israel and begin to deliver them from the hand of the Philistines. Manoah prayed and asked God, "teach us what we shall do unto the child that shall be born." God gave specific instructions concerning Manoah's wife and the baby to be born. Samson would follow the vow of a Nazarite as spelled out in Numbers 6:1-21.

---

1. How many years was Israel under the Philistines?

2. What was the name of Samson's father?

3. What would Samson be from the womb?

4. What was not to come upon Samson's head?

5. What did Manoah ask God to teach them concerning the child that would be born?

Important Truths:

God knows us before we are born.

God has a specific will for each of us.

Parents should seek God's help in rearing children.

Samson Kills a Thousand
Judges 15:14-16
(Study: Judges 15:1-20)

At various times, the Spirit of the Lord came upon Samson and he was able to do miraculous things like killing a lion, killing 30 Philistines, and breaking cords that had him tied. The Philistines came up to capture Samson and the children of Judah handed him over to them. When the Philistines shouted against him, the Spirit of God came upon him again, and he picked up a jawbone of a donkey and killed a thousand Philistines. Samson was faint from the battle and thought he would die for thirst, but God clave a hollow place in the jawbone that had water in it. Samson drank the water and was revived.

1. Where was Samson when the Philistines shouted against him?

2. Who gave Samson to the Philistines?

3. What did Samson use to kill the Philistines?

4. How many Philistines did Samson kill?

5. From what did Samson drink water?

Important Truths:

The Spirit of God on a person can help him do the miraculous.

God can use the insignificant to do the impossible.

God provides what we need.

Samson and Delilah
Judges 16:15-17
(Study: Judges 16:4-31)

Samson was a judge of Israel for 20 years. He is mentioned in Hebrews 11 as a hero of faith. Yet, Samson had a fleshly weakness, a lust for women. Delilah was a Philistine that was hired by lords of the Philistines to find out the secret to Samson's great strength. Three times Samson lied to Delilah about his strength, but finally told her "I have been a Nazarite unto God from my mother's womb: if I be shaven, then my strength will go from me, and I shall become weak, and be like any other man." Delilah had Samson's head shaven while he slept on her lap. The Philistines came and bound Samson and put out his eyes and put him in prison.

---

1. How many times did Samson lie to Delilah?

2. Delilah pressed Samson daily with her what?

3. What was Samson from the womb?

4. Who hired Delilah?

5. What did the Philistines do to Samson?

Important Truths:

Run from your temptation.

Sin blinds us to the truth.

There are consequences to sin.

Laish, Quiet & Secure
Judges 18:7-9
(Study: Judges 18:1-31)

In those days, there was no king in Israel, and the tribe of Dan sought more land for their inheritance. So, the Danites sent out five men to search the land for them. These spies came upon a city named Laish, that was quiet and secure. The city had no magistrate and no business with anyone. The spies saw that it was a good land and that the people in it would be an easy prey. Six hundred men returned with their weapons of war and the five spies to destroy and take the city of Laish. Since Laish had no leader and no business with anyone, they were killed and the city was burned with fire. The tribe of Dan moved there and called the city Dan after the name of their father.

---

1. What did Laish not have to put them to shame?

2. What did Laish not have with any man?

3. How many men spied out Laish?

4. How many men fought against Laish?

5. To what was the city of Laish's name changed?

Important Truths:

No man is an island to himself.

Leaders and restraint are for our protection.

A greedy person does not care from whom he takes.

No King in Israel
Judges 21:23-25
(Study: Judges 21:1-25)

This Bible story is only one verse long, but is described throughout the entire book of Judges. Twice in the book of Judges, God said, "In those days there was no king in Israel: every man did that which was right in his own eyes." The doings of Israel mentioned in the book of Judges show seven cycles of apostasy. The children of Israel would sin, God would judge them, they would cry to God for forgiveness, and then God would deliver them. The reason for their falling away from God is because there was no leader and every one would do what was right in his own eyes.

---

1. What was not in Israel in those days?

2. What did every man do?

3. Israel fell away from God how many times?

4. What was the cycle that Israel repeated in the book of Judges?

5. Why did Israel fall away?

Important Truths:

Good leadership is very important.

What is right in your own eyes is not always right.

God forgives and delivers.

Elimelech Leaves Judah
Ruth 1:1-3
(Study: Ruth 1:1-7)

Elimelech lived in the days of the judges when every man did that which was right in his own eyes. There was a famine in Bethlehem-Judah and Elimelech decided to move his family to Moab for a time. That one decision to leave the Promised Land would cost him. His wife's name was Naomi and his two sons were Mahlon and Chilion. While in Moab, Mahlon and Chilion married Orpah and Ruth. During the ten years they sojourned there, Elimelech and his two sons died and left Naomi, Orpah, and Ruth widows. Naomi decided to return to Judah because she heard "how that the LORD had visited his people in giving them bread."

1. Why did Elimelech leave Bethlehem-Judah?

2. How long was Elimelech's family in Moab?

3. Who died in Moab?

4. Who did Elimelech's sons marry?

5. Why did Naomi return to Judah?

Important Truths:

Famine can come even in the place of God's will.

One bad decision can affect a lot of people.

Always go back to the place of God's blessing.

Ruth Chooses God
Ruth 1:15-17
(Study: Ruth 1:1-22)

Naomi lost her husband and two sons in Moab after sojourning there ten years. She decided to go back home to Bethlehem. Naomi told her daughters-in-law, Orpah and Ruth to go back to their mother's house instead of returning with her to the land of Israel. Orpah went back, but Ruth clave to her mother-in-law. Ruth chose Naomi, Naomi's people, and Naomi's God. When Naomi saw that Ruth was "stedfastly minded to go with her, then she left speaking unto her." Then the two of them returned to Bethlehem in the beginning of barley harvest.

---

1. How many years was Naomi in Moab?

2. Who chose to stay in Moab?

3. Who was stedfastly minded to go with Naomi?

4. What three things did Ruth choose?

5. To what city did Naomi return?

Important Truths:

You always lose when living in the world.

The right choice is not always easy.

God is more important than family.

Ruth Gleans in Boaz's Field
Ruth 2:11-13
(Study: Ruth 2:1-23)

After Naomi and Ruth returned to Bethlehem, Ruth went out to work to provide food for the two of them. Ruth looked for a field from which she could pick up the leftovers that would have been dropped or left by the reapers. Ruth began gleaning in a field owned by Boaz, who was of the kindred of Elimelech, her deceased father-in-law. When Boaz saw her, he treated her kindly. He gave her water and food, and told his servants to let some fall on purpose for her to glean. Ruth "kept fast by the maidens of Boaz to glean unto the end of barley harvest and of wheat harvest; and dwelt with her mother-in-law."

---

1. In whose field did Ruth glean?

2. Who said, "the LORD recompense thy work?"

3. To whom was Boaz related?

4. Under whose wings did Ruth come to trust?

5. What did Boaz tell his servants to do for Ruth?

Important Truths:

God will lead us to the right place.

Hard work always pays off.

God gives to us on purpose.

Boaz Marries Ruth
Ruth 4:13-15
(Study: Ruth 3:1-4:22)

Boaz was the kinsmen redeemer that married Ruth. He told Ruth, "all the city of my people doth know that thou art a virtuous woman." Boaz went up to the gate of the city and sat down with ten elders of the city to purchase the land of Naomi and to marry Ruth the Moabite. There was one kinsman closer and more eligible to buy the property, but he refused when he found out he would have to marry Ruth to get it. Boaz took Ruth as his wife and they had a son named Obed, who would be the grandfather of King David.

---

1. Ruth was better than what to Naomi?

2. What did all the city know about Ruth?

3. What was the name of Ruth's son?

4. Who was Obed's grandson?

5. Who does the Bible say that Ruth loved?

Important Truths:

Jesus is the believer's Kinsman Redeemer.

Virtue pays off.

God is not a respecter of persons.

Hannah's Promise

I Samuel 1:10-12

(Study: I Samuel 1:1-20)

Hannah was married to a man named Elkanah. Hannah wanted children very much, "but the LORD had shut up her womb." Every year Elkanah would go up to Shiloh to worship and sacrifice unto the Lord. Every year Hannah would weep and not eat while in Shiloh because of her grief of having no children. Hannah went to pray unto the Lord at the temple. She vowed a vow to God that if He gave her a son, she would "give him unto the LORD all the days of his life." God answered her prayer and she gave birth to a boy named Samuel.

---

1. To whom was Hannah married?

2. Why could Hannah not have children?

3. Why did Elkanah take his family to Shiloh every year?

4. Who was the answer to Hannah's prayer?

5. Who watched Hannah vow to God?

Important Truths:

Burdens can be turned into blessings!

Faith promise giving is important.

God gives children.

The Birth of Samuel
I Samuel 1:26-28
(Study: I Samuel 1:19-28)

Samuel's name means asked of God. Hannah named him Samuel because she knew that he was a direct answer to her prayer and promise to God. After Samuel was born, Hannah did not go up to the yearly sacrifice in Shiloh until Samuel was weaned. The year finally came that Hannah brought Samuel to the house of the Lord in Shiloh to stay there and serve God. Samuel was very young when Hannah brought him to Eli the priest to stay and serve at the house of God. Hannah told Eli, "I have lent him to the LORD; as long as he liveth he shall be lent to the LORD." Samuel grew up with Eli in the temple and worshipped and served the Lord there.

---

1. What does Samuel's name mean?

2. Where did Hannah take Samuel to live?

3. With whom did Samuel go to live?

4. For how long did Hannah give Samuel to God?

5. Where did Samuel worship the Lord?

Important Truths:

Children should be given to the Lord.

Children can worship the Lord.

Children can be taught to serve the Lord.

Eli's Sons
I Samuel 2:22-24

(Study: I Samuel 2:12-36)

Eli was the high priest of Israel, and he had two sons named Hophni and Phinehas. Eli's sons were priests that made themselves vile and knew not the Lord. They caused the children of Israel to abhor the offering of the Lord. God warned Eli of their evil doings, but he would not do anything about it. Eli honored his sons above God, and would therefore lose the priesthood and his sons would die. God told Eli, "them that honour me I will honour, and they that despise me shall be lightly esteemed."

---

1. What position did Eli hold?

2. What were the names of Eli's sons?

3. What did Eli's sons make the Lord's people to do?

4. Was Eli young or old when his sons did evil?

5. What did God say would happen to the person that honored Him?

Important Truths:

People can minister, but still not know God.

Position in life does not exclude you from the consequences of sin.

Never put family before God.

Call of Samuel
I Samuel 3:8-10
(Study: I Samuel 3:1-21)

Samuel ministered unto the Lord as a child before the priest Eli. One night, Samuel went to bed and heard a voice call him and he went to Eli to see what he wanted. After this happened three times, Eli realized it was the Lord calling Samuel. The next time God called Samuel's name, Samuel responded, "Speak; for thy servant heareth." God revealed to Samuel the judgment that was coming against the house of Eli for the sins of his sons that he would not restrain. Samuel continued to grow and the Lord was with him, and all Israel knew that he was established to be a prophet of God.

1. How many times did God call out to Samuel?

2. To whom did Samuel minister before?

3. When did Samuel begin ministering unto the Lord?

4. How did Samuel answer God?

5. What did God reveal to Samuel?

Important Truths:

Children can be called to serve the Lord.

God speaks to children.

We should be sensitive to God speaking to us.

The Ark of God Taken
I Samuel 4:9-11
(Study: I Samuel 4:1-6:21)

The Philistines came up against the Israelites to battle. So, the Israelites went and got the Ark of the Covenant and brought it to the battlefield as if it would fight for them. The Ark of the Covenant was a piece of furniture in the tabernacle that housed the Ten Commandments and was a symbol of God's presence for Israel. During the battle, 30,000 Israelites were killed, Hophni and Phinehas were killed, and the ark of God was taken. When Eli the high priest, who judged Israel 40 years, heard the Ark of the Covenant was taken, he fell backward, broke his neck, and died. When Phinehas' wife heard the Ark was taken, she named her newborn son "Ichabod" meaning the glory is departed.

---

1. Who came to fight against the Israelites?

2. What did Israel think would fight for them?

3. What did the Ark of the Covenant contain?

4. How many Israelites died in the battle?

5. How many years did Eli judge Israel?

Important Truths:

God is not an object, but a Person.

God judges sin.

God's glory is departed when we sin.

The Stone of Ebenezer
I Samuel 7:11-13
(Study: I Samuel 7:1-17)

Samuel the prophet told the children of Israel, "If ye do return unto the LORD with all your hearts, then put away the strange gods and Ashtaroth from among you, and prepare your hearts unto the LORD, and serve him only: and he will deliver you out of the hand of the Philistines." So they obeyed and put away the false idols and gathered together to pray unto the Lord. The Philistines heard they had gathered and came up against them to battle. However, the Lord thundered on the Philistines and they were smitten before Israel. Samuel set up a stone as a memorial for their victory and he called it "Ebenezer" meaning God helped us.

1. What prophet told Israel to return to God?

2. What did Israel do to show their obedience?

3. What did God do for Israel?

4. What does Ebenezer mean?

5. How long was God's hand against the Philistines?

Important Truths:

God keeps His promises.

God will have no other gods before Him.

The Lord is our Help!

Samuel Makes His Sons Judges
I Samuel 8:1-3
(Study: I Samuel 8:1-6)

Samuel was an amazing man of God. He was born out of the prayers of his mother. He served God and was spoken to by God as a child. All Israel knew he was established to be the prophet of the Lord. God's hand was against the Philistines all the days of Samuel's life. "Samuel judged Israel all the days of his life." When Samuel was old, he made his sons judges over Israel. Unfortunately, his sons did not have the same character or spirituality that their father had. Because Samuel's sons perverted judgement by taking bribes, the children of Israel asked for a king, so they could be like all the other nations.

1. Who were Samuel's sons?

2. Who made Samuel's sons judges?

3. Samuel's sons turned aside after what?

4. How long did Samuel judge Israel?

5. What did Samuel's sons take that caused them to pervert judgment?

Important Truths:

Children do not always follow in their father's steps.

Fathers cannot make their children serve God.

Money has ruined a lot of good people.

Israel Chooses a King
I Samuel 8:6-8
(Study: I Samuel 8:6-22)

After Samuel made his sons judges, the people came to him and asked for a king to rule over them. They used the excuse that his sons did not walk in his ways. It displeased Samuel that they asked for a king, so he went to God with the matter. God told him to do it and that they had not rejected Samuel, but that they rejected God from reigning over them. Samuel told the children of Israel the manner of this king they wanted. He would take from them their sons, daughters, fields, servants, animals, and a tenth of their seed and sheep. He warned them that they "shall be his servants," and that they would cry out to God because of the request.

---

1. Who did Israel reject from reigning over them?

2. When Israel forsook God, whom did they serve?

3. What would their king take from them?

4. What would Israel do after getting a king?

5. Who did they blame for asking to have a king?

Important Truths:

You might get what you ask for, but lose what you have.

God should be the King of our lives.

Fleshly kings will take from us, not give to us.

Samuel Tells the Way
I Samuel 9:6-8
(Study: I Samuel 9:1-27)

Samuel the prophet was also called the Seer. Saul was sent out by his father to find some donkeys that were lost. Saul and the servant that went with him could not find them. After three days, they were about to go back home, but decided to go see the Seer to tell them the way home. The servant knew that the man of God could show them the way that they should go. After finding Samuel, he assured them that the donkeys that were lost, were found, and that God had a bigger plan for Saul. Samuel not only showed them their way, but he also told them the Word of God.

---

1. What was Samuel also called?

2. What kind of man was Samuel?

3. What would they give Samuel for showing them the way?

4. How long were the donkeys lost?

5. Samuel not only showed them the way, but also what else?

Important Truths:

The man of God can show you God's way.

There are no accidents with God.

God can use circumstances to lead us.

Saul Chosen to Be King
I Samuel 10:6-8
(Study: I Samuel 10:1-27)

Saul was chosen by God to be the first king of Israel. The prophet Samuel told Saul that God had chosen him and anointed him with oil to be captain over God's inheritance. Saul had the Spirit of the Lord come upon him and he was turned into another man. Samuel gathered Israel to Mizpeh to reveal their first king to them. Yet when Samuel said it was Saul, they could not find him because he had hidden himself among the stuff. When Saul was found and came to the people, he stood head and shoulders above them. Then all the people shouted "God save the king."

---

1. Who told Saul he would be king?

2. What was Saul anointed with to be king?

3. Where did Israel gather to meet their king?

4. What did Saul do when Samuel told the people who their king would be?

5. What happened to Saul when the Spirit of God came upon him?

Important Truths:

God chooses to promote individuals to leadership.

Humility is key for any leader.

The Spirit of God will turn you into another man.

The Good and Right Way
I Samuel 12:23-25
(Study: I Samuel 12:1-25)

After King Saul's first battle, the children of Israel came to Gilgal to renew the kingdom before Samuel. Samuel rehearsed the history of Israel and the leaders that God gave them: men like Moses, Aaron, Gideon, Jephthah, and even Samuel himself. Samuel told the people that God would send thunder and rain to show their great wickedness in asking a king. The people were afraid, but Samuel told them to fear not and to make sure they walked in the good and right way. The way was to fear God, serve Him with all their hearts, and consider how great things God had done for them.

---

1. Who were some of Israel's leaders?

2. Samuel considered not doing what, a sin?

3. What is the good and right way?

4. What would happen to Israel if they did wickedly?

5. What was Israel's great wickedness?

Important Truths:

God should be our only King.

God uses men to lead us.

There is a good and right way.

Saul Rejected as King
I Samuel 13:12-14
(Study: I Samuel 13:1-23)

After Saul had been king for two years, the Philistines came up against him with an army "as the sand which is on the sea shore in multitude." Saul waited for Samuel for seven days to come and make supplication for him before the Lord. When he thought Samuel was not coming, Saul offered a burnt offering unto the Lord that only the priest was to do. Samuel came as soon as Saul made the offering and told him, "Thou hast done foolishly: thou hast not kept the commandment of the LORD...But now thy kingdom shall not continue: the LORD hath sought him a man after his own heart."

---

1. Who came to fight against Israel?

2. What did Saul do wrong?

3. What was the Lord seeking?

4. How many days had Saul waited for Samuel?

5. What would God have done for Saul if he had not done wrong?

Important Truths:

You cannot justify wrong with right.

Pressure can make or break us.

Nobody is irreplaceable.

Jonathan's Armourbearer
I Samuel 14:5-7
(Study: I Samuel 14:1-14)

Jonathan was King Saul's son and a commander of Saul's army. When the Philistines came up with a great army against Israel, King Saul tarried under a tree. Jonathan said to his armourbearer "there is no restraint to the LORD to save by many or by few." His armourbearer answered Jonathan, "Do all that is in thine heart…behold, I am with thee." Jonathan attacked the Philistines with his armourbearer and they killed twenty Philistines. This first step of faith would give them a great victory. It all started with the loyalty, faith, and fight of an unnamed armourbearer who was willing to follow and fight with the man he served.

1. Who was the enemy fighting Israel?

2. What was King Saul doing?

3. Who did Jonathan ask to help him?

4. How many Philistines did they kill together?

5. There is no restraint for God to save by what?

Important Truths:

God's men need help.

Great victories are won by the unknown.

Servants can encourage or discourage leadership.

Jonathan Makes a Difference
I Samuel 14:15-17
(Study: I Samuel 14:15-52)

Jonathan and his armourbearer were the cause of a great victory over the Philistines. Even though they were completely outnumbered, Jonathan trusted in God and went to fight against the Philistines with just his armourbearer. Their step of faith would begin a domino effect that caused the Philistines to be defeated. After Jonathan's attack, the Philistines began killing each other. When Saul and his men came to the fight, then the Israelites that were with the Philistines before, turned and fought, and also the Israelites that were hiding, came and fought. All of this happened because Jonathan wanted to make a difference.

---

1. Who went with Jonathan to battle?

2. Who beat down one another?

3. What "quaked" during this battle?

4. How did Saul know Jonathan and his armourbearer were gone?

5. The Philistines were defeated because of whose step of faith?

Important Truths:

One person can make a difference.

Others are watching you.

One plus God makes the majority.

Saul's Incomplete Obedience
I Samuel 15:13-15
(Study: I Samuel 15:1-15)

King Saul was told by God to utterly destroy the Amalekites for what they did to Israel when they came out of Egypt. Saul took an army of 210,000 to fight against the Amalekites. He won the battle, but did not utterly destroy them, and spared King Agag and the animals that were good. When Saul met Samuel, he said to him, "I have performed the commandment of the LORD." Yet in actuality he only did in part because he did not destroy all, like God commanded. Saul blamed his incomplete obedience on the people of Israel for sparing the best of the sheep and oxen. He also justified his disobedience by saying they were going to offer the animals they spared as a sacrifice to the Lord.

1. Whom did God say to destroy?

2. How many were in Saul's army?

3. Who did Saul blame for his disobedience?

4. Who confronted Saul for his disobedience?

5. Which king did Saul spare?

Important Truths:

Incomplete obedience is disobedience.

It is never right to do wrong in order to do right.

Don't blame others for your disobedience.

Samuel Reproves Saul
I Samuel 15:22-24
(Study: I Samuel 15:16-35)

God told Saul to utterly destroy the Amalekites, but instead he spared King Agag and the good animals. Saul thought he could partially obey God, and it would be alright. Samuel came to him and reproved him for his disobedience. Samuel told Saul the root cause for his disobedience was pride. Saul tried to justify his wrong doing by saying he spared the animals to offer as sacrifices for God. Samuel said, "to obey is better than sacrifice." Because of Saul's rebellion, stubbornness, and disobedience, God rejected Saul from being king, and gave the kingship to another man.

1. What is better than sacrifice?

2. What should Saul have done?

3. What sin is rebellion like?

4. Stubbornness is as what two things?

5. What did Saul reject that caused God to reject him as king?

Important Truths:

To obey is better than sacrifice.

Disobedience causes us to lose out on God's blessings.

Reproof brings things to light in our lives.

David Chosen to Be King
I Samuel 16:11-13
(Study: I Samuel 16:1-13)

Saul had disobeyed God and the Lord looked for a man after his own heart to be the next king. God led the prophet Samuel to Jesse and his sons to find such a one. "But the LORD said unto Samuel, Look not on his countenance, or on the height of his stature; because I have refused him: for the LORD seeth not as man seeth; for man looketh on the outward appearance, but the LORD looketh on the heart." One by one, Jesse's sons came before Samuel only to find that they were not the one. Samuel asked Jesse if he had any more sons, and he responded that there was still the youngest. His name was David and he was keeping the sheep. David was the one God had chosen to be king!

1. What kind of man was God looking for to be king?

2. On what does God look?

3. How was David's countenance described?

4. What came upon David?

5. What was David found doing?

Important Truths:

God is the One who promotes man.

God looks at the heart.

God has a plan for everyone.

God Departs from Saul
I Samuel 16:14-16
(Study: I Samuel 16:14-23)

King Saul, because of his pride and disobedience, lost the Spirit of God upon his life. With the absence of the Holy Spirit, Saul had an evil spirit trouble him. Saul's servants recommended he find a man that could play a harp when Saul was troubled, in order to make him well. David was selected to play before Saul. One of Saul's servants said that David was "cunning in playing, and a mighty valiant man, and a man of war, and prudent in matters, and a comely person, and the LORD is with him." David played the harp and Saul was refreshed and the evil spirit departed from him.

1. What troubled King Saul?

2. The Lord was with whom?

3. Why did Saul lose the Spirit of God?

4. What refreshed Saul?

5. Music caused what to depart from Saul?

Important Truths:

Music can refresh you.

Staying filled with the Spirit keeps us from trouble.

A man's gift will bring him before great men.

Goliath Defies Israel
I Samuel 17:8-10
(Study: I Samuel 17:1-14)

The Philistines gathered their armies against the Israelites in the valley of Elah. The champion of the Philistines, Goliath, came out and told Israel to choose a man to represent their nation to fight him. Goliath was a giant of a man, at least nine feet tall. A fight to the death would decide who should serve whom. If Goliath won, then Israel would serve the Philistines, and if the man who fought Goliath won, then the Philistines would serve Israel. The problem was that no one wanted to fight the giant Goliath. Saul and all Israel were "dismayed, and greatly afraid" by the words of Goliath.

---

1. Who was the Philistine's champion?

2. In what valley did they come to fight?

3. How tall was Goliath?

4. What would decide who would serve whom?

5. What did Goliath say to give him?

Important Truths:

It doesn't matter how big the enemy is, God is bigger.

Actions speak louder than words.

There are not very many real men.

David Had a Cause
I Samuel 17:28-30
(Study: I Samuel 17:15-30)

David was at home with his father Jesse. David was keeping the sheep when Goliath defied God and challenged Israel. Jesse sent David to the battle with food for his brothers and instructions to see how they were and to take their pledge. When David arrived where the battle between Israel and the Philistines was taking place, he heard Goliath's challenge for a man to fight him. The men around David told him how the king would reward the man who fought and killed Goliath. Eliab, David's eldest brother was angry with David's inquiry of killing Goliath and rebuked him. David said, "Is there not a cause?"

1. Who was David's father?

2. Who was David's older brother?

3. Who was defying God and Israel?

4. What did David say in response to Eliab's rebuke?

5. What was David's job at home?

Important Truths:

There will be those who say it can't be done.

"Is there not a cause?"

Age does not always equal wisdom.

Thou Art but a Youth
I Samuel 17:33-35
(Study: I Samuel 17:31-39)

David told King Saul that he would fight Goliath when no one else would. Saul told David he was not able to fight Goliath because he was just a youth. David told Saul of the day that he fought a lion and bear to protect the sheep and how God delivered them into his hand, and that God would do the same with Goliath. Saul tried to give David his armor, but David refused it because he had not proved it. David did not allow his youth or inexperience as a soldier to keep him from doing what God wanted him to do. God had already prepared David for Goliath by having him fight a lion and a bear.

---

1. Who told David he was not able to fight?

2. Why did Saul tell David he could not fight Goliath?

3. What enemies did David fight before Goliath?

4. What had David not proven?

5. How many others were willing to fight?

Important Truths:

Young people can do great things for God.

There will always be those who discourage others from serving God.

Early battles in life prepare us for bigger ones later.

David and Goliath
I Samuel 17:49-51
(Study: I Samuel 17:40-58)

David took his staff, shepherd's bag, scrip, sling, and five smooth stones to fight Goliath. When Goliath saw David, he noticed he was but a youth and cursed him. Yet David said to Goliath "Thou comest to me with a sword, and with a spear, and with a shield: but I come to thee in the name of the LORD." David ran toward Goliath and took a stone from his bag and slung it into the forehead of Goliath which caused him to fall flat on his face. Then David ran and stood upon Goliath and took his sword and cut off his head. When the Philistine army saw their champion was dead, they fled and the army of Israel pursued after them.

1. How many stones did David take with him?

2. Where did David sling the stone?

3. What did the Philistines do when Goliath died?

4. What did David use to kill Goliath?

5. What did Israel do when David killed Goliath?

Important Truths:

Courage comes from a faith in God.

With God you can defeat any giant.

Use what you have to serve God.

Jonathan and David
I Samuel 18:1-3
(Study: I Samuel 18:1-4)

After David killed Goliath, King Saul set David over the men of war. Jonathan the son of King Saul, loved David as his own soul. Jonathan made a covenant with David because he loved him as his own soul. As a token of friendship, Jonathan gave David his robe, garments, sword, bow, and girdle. The two of them would be friends for a lifetime. Even when Jonathan's own father hated and tried to kill David, Jonathan stayed true to David and protected him. Jonathan was a godly friend. I Samuel 23:16 says that Jonathan "went to David into the wood, and strengthened his hand in God."

1. Who loved David as his own soul?

2. What did Jonathan give David as a token of his friendship?

3. Jonathan strengthened David's hand in what?

4. Who hated and tried to kill David?

5. What did Jonathan make with David because he loved him?

Important Truths:

A friend can make or break you.

Godly friends point you to God.

Value a real friend.

Jealousy of Saul
I Samuel 18:6-8
(Study: I Samuel 18:5-19)

After David killed Goliath, King Saul set him over the men of war. After David returned from a slaughter of the Philistines, the women of Israel met King Saul with singing that was quite disturbing to him. They sang "Saul hath slain his thousands, and David his ten thousands." Saul was very wroth and displeased because the Israelite women ascribed unto David ten thousand and only thousands to him. This jealousy caused him to eye David from that day forward. Saul tried to kill David by casting a javelin at him, while David played the harp for him. Saul was afraid of David because God was with him and David behaved himself wisely.

1. Of whom was Saul jealous?

2. What increased Saul's jealousy?

3. How did Saul try to kill David?

4. Why was Saul afraid of David?

5. How did David behave himself?

Important Truths:

Jealousy is the rage of a man.

Don't listen to everything said about you or others.

The best defense to jealousy, is having God with you.

David Marries Michal
I Samuel 18:20-22
(Study: I Samuel 18:20-30)

King Saul was afraid of David and wanted him to die. He hoped that David would be killed by the hand of the Philistines. In hopes of him fighting for the kingdom, and being killed in battle, he promised him his eldest daughter Merab. At the time he should have married her, Saul changed his mind and gave her to another. Michal, Saul's daughter, loved David. Saul said he would give her to David to wife that she might be a snare to him and the hand of the Philistines may be against him. After Saul gave Michal to David in marriage, he "saw and knew that the Lord was with David and that Michal, Saul's daughter, loved him."

1. Who did Saul promise to David first?

2. Who loved David?

3. What did Saul know?

4. What did Saul want Michal to be toward to David?

5. Who was Saul hoping would kill David?

Important Truths:

God knows whom you should marry.

What man means for evil, God can turn to good.

It is best to have the Lord with you when choosing a spouse.

Jonathan Intercedes
I Samuel 19:4-6
(Study: I Samuel 19:1-10)

King Saul continued to hate David and wanted to kill him. Jonathan, Saul's son loved David and protected him. When Saul talked to Jonathan and his servants about killing David, Jonathan told David to hide himself while he interceded for him before his father, in order for his life to be spared. "Saul hearkened unto the voice of Jonathan: and Saul sware, As the LORD liveth, he shall not be slain." Yet it was not long after that when David won another victory against the Philistines, and Saul's jealousy had him casting javelins at David again.

---

1. Who wanted to kill David?

2. Who tried to save David's life?

3. What did Saul cast at David?

4. What did Saul promise?

5. What did David do that caused Saul to become jealous of him again?

Important Truths:

"A friend loveth at all times."

"Jealousy is cruel as the grave."

Learn how to fix offences.

Michal Protects David
I Samuel 19:11-13
(Study: I Samuel 19:11-17)

Michal was David's wife, but she was also Saul's daughter. Michal had to decide if she would listen to her father or protect her husband. She made the right choice, and let David out a window so he could escape. Saul sent messengers to get David and Michal told them he was sick. Saul told his messengers to bring David to him in his bed so he could slay him. When Saul found out that Michal protected David he said to her "Why hast thou deceived me so, and sent away mine enemy, that he is escaped? And Michal answered Saul, He said unto me, Let me go; why should I kill thee?" Michal protected her husband.

---

1. Who was David's wife?

2. Who wanted to kill David?

3. What did Michal tell the messengers when they came for David?

4. How did David escape?

5. Who did Saul say was his enemy?

Important Truths:

God established the leave and cleave principle of marriage.

Protect your spouse.

Some choices with family are hard to make.

Jonathan & David's Covenant
I Samuel 20:15-17
(Study: I Samuel 20:1-17)

Once again, Saul was out to kill David. David went to Jonathan and told him of his father's evil intent to kill him. Jonathan did not believe that his father would do that without telling him of his plans. Yet, David knew, that because he found grace in Jonathan's eyes, that his father had hid it from him. David asked Jonathan to give him leave from a dinner he would be expected to be at, to see if his father was upset for his absence, as a sign of his father's desire to kill him. Jonathan gave him leave and made a covenant with David that he would show kindness to his household forever. This covenant between the two of them was because Jonathan loved David as he loved his own soul.

---

1. Who made a covenant with David?

2. From whom did Saul hide his intent to kill David?

3. In whose eyes did David find grace?

4. For how long was the covenant good?

5. To whom would David show kindness?

> **Important Truths:**
>
> Friendship is important.
>
> A covenant of love is not easily broken.
>
> Friendships can be stronger than other relationships.

David Runs from Saul
I Samuel 21:10-12
(Study: I Samuel 21:1-15)

David was afraid of Saul and ran for his life. David went to hide with a Philistine king named Achish, in the city of Gath. David went from fearing Saul to being very afraid of Achish. The servants of Achish said to him, "Is not this David the king of the land?" Of whom they sang, "Saul hath slain his thousands, and David his ten thousands?" David knew he was in enemy territory and feared for his life. David changed his behavior and acted like a mad man who had lost his mind. Achish did not worry about David's presence in Gath because of his acting as if he were insane.

---

1. Of whom was David fearful?

2. Of whom was David very afraid?

3. Who was Achish?

4. How did David change his behavior?

5. Who did the servants of Achish say was the king of the land?

Important Truths:

You will always be worse when you leave the will of God.

Don't go to the world for help.

The fear of man brings a snare.

The Prophet Gad Warns David
I Samuel 22:3-5
(Study: I Samuel 22:1-5)

David ran for his life from Saul and escaped to the cave of Adullam. Four hundred men gathered unto David for him to be their captain. This band of men is described as distressed, discontented, and in debt. David protected his father and mother by taking them to the king of Moab and asking for his parents to stay with him until he knew what God would do for him. In the midst of all this, the prophet Gad, told David that he should stay in the land of Judah. Previously, David went into Philistine territory for protection from Saul. David followed the prophet's advice and dwelt in Judah in the forest of Hareth.

1. How many men followed David?

2. What kind of men were they?

3. To what king did David take his parents?

4. What prophet warned David?

5. Where did the prophet tell David to stay?

Important Truths:

Take care of your parents!

People who help you, need your help too!

Listen to the man of God!

Doeg
I Samuel 22:9-11
(Study: I Samuel 22:7-23)

David was on the run from Saul and stopped in the city of Nob and spoke with Ahimelech the priest who gave him bread and a sword for his journey (I Samuel 21:6-9). Ahimelech did not know that David was running from Saul. One of Saul's servants named Doeg was there that day and told Saul what Ahimelech had done. Saul told Doeg to kill Ahimelech and 85 priests of his father's house. He even had killed all those in the city of Nob, "both men and women, children and sucklings, and oxen, and asses, and sheep." Saul's jealousy of David caused him to murder innocent people. Abiathar, Ahimelech's son, escaped Saul's wrath and fled to David, who kept him safe.

---

1. What priest did Saul have killed?

2. Who did Saul tell to kill the priests?

3. How many priests did Doeg kill?

4. In what city did Saul have everyone killed?

5. Who escaped Saul's wrath?

Important Truths:

Jealousy is the rage of a man.

"The words of a talebearer are as wounds."

"Death and life are in the power of the tongue."

David Saves the City of Keilah
I Samuel 23:2-4
(Study: I Samuel 23:1-13)

David heard that the Philistines were fighting against Keilah, a city of Judah. So David inquired of the Lord whether or not he should go and help the city fight against the Philistines. The Lord said to help, but David's men were afraid to do so. David inquired again, and God promised David that He would deliver the Philistines into his hand. So David and his men went to Keilah and smote the Philistines "with a great slaughter," and saved the inhabitants of Keilah. After their victory, David and his 600 men departed from Keilah because Saul was coming to Keilah to try to kill David.

---

1. How many men did David have with him?

2. Who was fighting against Keilah?

3. Who was afraid to go fight at Keilah?

4. Who wanted to get David at Keilah?

5. Who told David to "save Keilah"?

Important Truths:

God uses people to protect us.

God will direct us if we will inquire of Him.

Satan likes to show his face after great victories.

David Strengthened in God
I Samuel 23:15-17
(Study: I Samuel 23:14-18)

"David...remained in a mountain in the wilderness of Ziph. And Saul sought him every day, but God delivered him not into his hand." Even though Saul sought to kill David, Jonathan, Saul's son, sought to encourage David. Jonathan went to David where he was hiding from Saul and "strengthened his hand in God." Jonathan knew that David was to be the next king of Israel and encouraged him by telling him so. David and Jonathan made a covenant that day between the two of them. Their friendship was rooted and grounded in God and His will for both of their lives. Jonathan's words of encouragement were for David to keep his hand in God's hand.

---

1. Who sought to kill David every day?

2. Who delivered David from Saul?

3. Jonathan strengthened David's hand in Whom?

4. Who did Jonathan say would be king?

5. Who else knew David would be the next king?

Important Truths:

Strengthening comes from having your hand in God's hand.

Real friends take you closer to God.

Even our enemies can only do what God will allow.

David Escapes Saul Again
I Samuel 23:26-28
(Study: I Samuel 23:19-29)

The Ziphites came to Saul and said, "Doth not David hide himself with us in strong holds in the wood…our part shall be to deliver him into the king's hand." So Saul and his men came after David and passed by them on one side of the mountain while David and his men were on the other side. Saul was very close to taking David, but the Lord delivered David. Saul received word that the Philistines had invaded the land and he was needed immediately. "Saul returned from pursuing David, and went against the Philistines." God kept David safe from Saul! Saul's plans against David could not defeat God's purpose for him.

---

1. Who told Saul where David was?

2. Where did Saul try to take David?

3. Who invaded the land?

4. What could Saul's plans not defeat?

5. Who kept David safe?

Important Truths:

Make sure you are on the right side.

Our plans should coincide with God's will.

It is God Who keeps us safe.

Don't Touch God's Anointed
I Samuel 24:5-7
(Study: I Samuel 24:1-22)

King Saul went to pursue after David with 3,000 men in the wilderness of Engedi. Saul went into a cave to rest, not knowing that David and his men were in the sides of the cave. David's men said to kill Saul, but David would not because Saul was the Lord's anointed. David cut a piece from Saul's garment and kept his men from killing Saul. When Saul arose to go his way, David followed him out of the cave and said to him, "the LORD had delivered thee to day into mine hand in the cave: and *some* bade *me* kill thee: but *mine eye* spared thee; and I said, I will not put forth mine hand against my lord; for he *is* the LORD'S anointed." Saul told David he was more righteous than himself.

1. How many men did Saul have with him?

2. Where did Saul go to rest?

3. Why would David not kill Saul?

4. Who told David to kill Saul?

5. What did David cut from Saul?

Important Truths:

You should not go against God's anointed.

"...Overcome evil with good." (Romans 12:21).

"...Love your enemies." (Matthew 5:44)

The Foolishness of Nabal
I Samuel 25:10-12
(Study: I Samuel 25:1-13)

Nabal was rightly named, as his name means fool. He was a rough, mean spirited man, who was "evil in his doings." David sent 10 of his servants to Nabal to ask for some help and sustenance for his men. David reminded Nabal that he had helped his servants in the past. Nabal railed on David's servants instead of helping them. Even Nabal's servants said of their master that "he is such a son of Belial, that a man cannot speak to him." When David heard what Nabal had done, he told his men to gird every man on his sword and to go with him against Nabal and his household.

---

1. What does Nabal's name mean?

2. How many men did David send to Nabal?

3. From whom did Nabal say David had broken away?

4. Who had David helped in the past?

5. Nabal's servants said Nabal was a son of whom?

Important Truths:

We should be kind to those who have helped us.

We are known by what we do.

Those who cannot be corrected, cannot be taught.

The Wisdom of Abigail
I Samuel 25:26-28
(Study: I Samuel 25:14-35)

Abigail was married to foolish Nabal. Yet, she is described in scripture as "a woman of good understanding, and of a beautiful countenance." Nabal refused to help David in his time of need, after David and his men had helped and protected Nabal's servants in the past. Because Nabal returned to David evil for good, David and his men set out to kill Nabal and his household. Abigail met David with food and supplies, and to offer an apology for her husband's foolishness. David acknowledged that God had sent Abigail to meet him, and blessed her for coming and keeping him from hurting her and Nabal's household.

---

1. Who was Abigail's husband?

2. How is Abigail described?

3. Nabal returned to David evil for what?

4. Who sent Abigail to David?

5. For whom did Abigail say David fought battles?

Important Truths:

Be careful whom you marry.

God sends people our way to encourage us to make right decisions.

Know how to say "I am sorry."

Nabal Gets What He Deserves
I Samuel 25:37-39
(Study: I Samuel 25:36-44)

Nabal railed on David's servants instead of helping them, after David and his men helped Nabal by protecting them in the past. David wanted to destroy Nabal and his household for his insult, but did not because of the intercession of his wife Abigail. When Abigail returned home, she told her husband the next day all that she had done to help and to apologize to David. When Nabal heard this, he became like a stone and within ten days, God killed him. David recognized that the reason Nabal died was because "the LORD hath returned the wickedness of Nabal upon his own head." David married Nabal's wise widow, Abigail.

---

1. Who asked David to pardon Nabal's insult?

2. Who killed Nabal?

3. God returned what to Nabal?

4. How long was Nabal like a stone?

5. Whom did David marry?

Important Truths:

God will reward us according to our righteousness or wickedness.

"Vengeance is mine,.. saith the Lord."

God blesses you when you do right.

David Spares Saul Again
I Samuel 26:9-11
(Study: I Samuel 26:1-25)

As in the past, Saul went out with 3,000 men to seek David in the wilderness. David went to where Saul had pitched his camp. While Saul lay asleep with his men about him, David and Abishai came unto him. God had put a deep sleep upon Saul and his men, so that they did not awaken. Abishai wanted to kill Saul, but David would not allow him to. David said to Abishai, "who can stretch forth his hand against the LORD's anointed, and be guiltless." They took Saul's spear and cruse of water and went to a hill far away. When David called out to Saul, he showed him the spear and cruse of water and told him how he had spared his life. Saul said to David, "I have played the fool, and have erred exceedingly."

1. How many men did Saul have with him?

2. Who did David take with him?

3. What did David take of Saul's?

4. What did God put on Saul's men?

5. Who said, "I have played the fool?"

Important Truths:

Don't touch God's anointed.

Look to God for deliverance.

Not everyone will think spiritually.

David Said in His Heart
I Samuel 27:1-3
(Study: I Samuel 27:1-12)

David was getting tired of Saul hunting him every day (I Samuel 23:14). Because of this, he allowed his heart to tell him what to do, and moved into Philistine territory. He knew that Saul would not hunt him in the land of his enemies. David, with his 600 men and their households, went to Gath and asked King Achish for a place to stay. Achish gave him a place called Ziklag to live in that was outside the royal city of Gath. Achish believed David and said, "He hath made his people Israel utterly to abhor him; therefore he shall be my servant for ever." David dwelt in the country of the Philistines for a year and four months.

---

1. Where did David go to flee from Saul?

2. What Philistine king gave David a place to live?

3. What city did David live in while in Philistine country?

4. How long was David in Philistine country?

5. How many men went with David?

Important Truths:

You cannot always follow your heart.

There is no way to get back lost time.

When you get out of God's will, you take others with you.

The Witch of Endor
I Samuel 28:7-9
(Study: I Samuel 28:1-14)

The Philistines came up against Israel with a large host and Saul was afraid. What made things worse was that Saul could get no direction from God, and Samuel, the man of God, was dead. So, Saul searched for one who could call up the dead by an evil spirit. He found such a witch at a place called Endor. At one time, Saul had put away from the land of Israel all witches and wizards. God told Israel in Leviticus 19:31 "Regard not them that have familiar spirits, neither seek after wizards, to be defiled by them: I am the LORD your God." Saul disobeyed God by going to the witch of Endor and asking her to call Samuel up from the dead.

---

1. Who came up against Israel?

2. From whom could Saul get no direction?

3. Where did Saul find one with an evil spirit?

4. Who did Saul want to see that was dead?

5. Whom had Saul put away from Israel?

Important Truths:

Christians should never deal with evil spirits.

The end does not justify the means.

Wrong does not change because of circumstances.

God Is Departed from Me
I Samuel 28:15-17
(Study: I Samuel 28:15-25)

Saul went to the witch of Endor to have her call up from the dead the prophet Samuel, so Saul could get some direction for the upcoming battle with the Philistines. Saul's dilemma was that God was departed from him and didn't answer him. Samuel told Saul that "the LORD is departed from thee and is become thine enemy." God departed because Saul obeyed not the voice of the Lord and executed not judgement against Amalek. Because of Saul's disobedience, God would deliver him, his sons, and the Israelites into the hand of the Philistines the next day.

---

1. Who was fighting against Israel?

2. In what two ways did Saul say that God would not answer him?

3. Who had become Saul's enemy?

4. To whom did God give Saul's kingdom?

5. Who else would feel the consequences of Saul's disobedience?

Important Truths:

You don't want God to depart from you.

Disobedience separates you from God.

Our choices always affect others.

Kept from Fighting
I Samuel 29:7-9
(Study: I Samuel 29:1-11)

David was living in Philistine country out of the will of God. When Achish, the king of Gath, went to war against Israel, he took David and his men with him. When the other lords of the Philistines saw David and his men, they refused to let them go to battle with them. They were afraid that David in the midst of battle would fight against them and for Israel. So David returned unto the land of the Philistines, while they went to fight against Israel. God intervened on David's behalf to keep him from having to fight against Israel.

---

1. Who was the king of Gath?

2. Who was said to be "as an angel of God?"

3. Who were the Philistines going to fight?

4. Where was David living at this time?

5. Who said that David and his men could not go to battle?

Important Truths:

You should not fight against brethren.

You pick what side you are on by who you hang with.

God can keep you from fighting.

Encouraged in the Lord
I Samuel 30:4-6
(Study: I Samuel 30:1-8)

After David was sent home by the Philistines, he came to Ziklag to find it burnt with fire. The Amalekites had invaded the land and taken the women and children as captives. David's men were so grieved by the loss of their sons and daughters that they spoke of stoning David. In the midst of David's home being burnt to the ground, his wives taken captive, and being greatly distressed, "David encouraged himself in the LORD his God." The first thing David did was to enquire with the Lord what to do. God told him to pursue the Amalekites and promised that he would recover all.

---

1. What city did David live in?

2. Who burned it to the ground?

3. Who spoke of stoning David?

4. Who did David encourage?

5. What was the first thing that David did after seeing what was done at Ziklag?

Important Truths:

Testing and trials come even to good people.

A believer's encouragement comes from God.

Grief can bring out the worst in people.

Those That Stay by the Stuff
I Samuel 30:22-24
(Study: I Samuel 30:9-31)

David was in pursuit of the Amalekites who burned Ziklag and took his wives captive. When David and his 600 men got to the brook Besor, 200 of his men were faint and could not go over the brook, so they stayed there by the stuff. David caught up with the Amalekites, smote them, recovered everything, and rescued his wives. David returned to the 200 men that were too faint to go with him. There were wicked men with David who said they should not get any of the spoil except their own wives and children and be gone. Yet, David said, "but as his part is that goeth down to the battle, so shall his part be that tarrieth by the stuff: they shall part alike."

1. How many stayed by the stuff?

2. Why did they stay back?

3. Who did David defeat?

4. Who did David say delivered the Amalekites?

5. What kind of men said not to give to those who tarried?

Important Truths:

Some people are needed on the home front.

It is selfish to not want to share.

Even good people can become faint.

Kindness to the Dead
I Samuel 31:11-13
(Study: I Samuel 31:1-13)

Saul and all the Israelites went to battle against the Philistines and lost. Saul and his sons and the soldiers with them were killed. The next day after the battle, the Philistines came to strip the slain of their armor and found Saul's body. They took his body and hung it on a wall in Beth-shan to show their victory. The valiant men of Jabesh-gilead came and took his body off the wall and buried him. David later said, "Blessed be ye of the LORD, that ye have shewed this kindness unto your lord, even unto Saul, and have buried him" (II Samuel 2:5).

---

1. Who was Saul fighting in battle?

2. What did the Philistines do with Saul's body?

3. Who took down Saul's body and buried him?

4. Who blessed them for burying Saul?

5. The men who buried Saul were described as what kind of men?

Important Truths:

Give honor to whom honor is due.

We should be respectful of those who pass away.

Sin has its consequences.

How Are the Mighty Fallen
II Samuel 1:25-27
(Study: II Samuel 1:1-27)

The Philistines came up against the Israelites and defeated them. David had just returned to Ziklag after destroying the Amalekites, who had burned his city. A young man, that identified himself as an Amalekite, came and told David in Ziklag how the battle against the Philistines fell out. He told him that Saul and Jonathan were dead and that Israel lost the battle. David asked him how he knew that Saul was dead, and he told him that Saul was wounded and asked him to kill him because he was in anguish. David had the Amalekite killed for touching God's anointed and lamented Saul and Jonathan's death. Three times David said of Saul and Jonathan, "How are the mighty fallen."

1. Who killed Saul?

2. Where was David when Saul died?

3. For whom was David distressed?

4. Why was the Amalekite killed?

5. Who were the mighty that fell?

Important Truths:

We should still respect those who resent us.

Even the mightiest can fall.

You should never be happy when your enemy falls.

David Made King of Judah
II Samuel 2:2-4
(Study: II Samuel 2:1-11)

After Saul was killed in battle with the Philistines, David enquired of the Lord what he should do. God told David to go up into Hebron, a city of Judah. So David took his wives and his men and their households and came into the cities of Hebron. Then the men of Judah came and anointed David to be king over the house of Judah. Yet, Abner, captain of Saul's host, took Ish-bosheth the son of Saul and made him king over all Israel. For seven years and six months David was king in Hebron over the house of Judah. David's first act as king was to requite the kindness of the men of Jabesh-gilead for their kindness to Saul.

1. God told David to go up to which city?

2. Who made David king?

3. Who became king over all Israel?

4. Who made Ish-bosheth king?

5. How long was David king in Hebron?

Important Truths:

Sometimes we have to wait for God's promises to be fulfilled.

Reward those who do right.

Lead those who want to follow.

Asahel Wouldn't Listen
II Samuel 2:21-23
(Study: II Samuel 2:12-32)

David was the king of Judah, while Ish-bosheth reigned over Israel. Joab was the captain of David's men, and Abner was the captain of Ish-bosheth's. Joab and Abner's men had a battle against one another in which Abner's army was put to the worse. Asahel, Joab's younger brother went after Abner in the battle and would not stop from following after him. Abner warned Asahel twice to go after someone else or he would have to kill him, but he would not listen. When Asahel refused to turn aside, Abner smote him with his spear and he died. That day in the battle twenty servants of David died, and 360 of Abner's men were killed.

1. Who was the captain of David's army?

2. Who was the captain of Ish-bosheth's army?

3. Who was Asahel?

4. Who did Asahel try to kill in battle?

5. How many times did Abner warn Asahel?

Important Truths:

Young people should listen to older people.

Wisdom is better than strength.

There is no remedy for repeatedly shunning reproof.

Fixing a Wrong Choice
II Samuel 3:17-19
(Study: II Samuel 3:1-21)

Abner was the one who made Ish-bosheth king over Israel when Saul was killed in battle (II Samuel 2:8-9). However, he knew that David was to be the next king, by his own admission. Abner said, "for the LORD hath spoken of David, saying, By the hand of my servant David I will save my people Israel." Yet, it wasn't until Ish-bosheth reproved Abner that he now wanted to put David as king. Abner came to David at Hebron to tell him that he would gather all Israel to make a league with him to make him king over all Israel. Abner should have done this in the first place.

1. Who sought David in times past to be king?

2. Who tried to fix a wrong choice?

3. Who reproved Abner?

4. Who said David would save Israel?

5. Where did Abner meet David?

Important Truths:

It is not too late to try to fix a wrong choice.

Some wrong choices cannot be changed.

Better to say, "thank God I did" instead of "Would God I had."

A Great Man Fallen
II Samuel 3:37-39
(Study: II Samuel 3:22-39)

Abner came to David at Hebron to discuss reuniting Judah and Israel under him as king. After they spoke, David sent him away in peace. Joab returned to Hebron shortly after Abner left, and was disturbed that David would have anything to do with Abner. Joab was bitter toward Abner for killing his brother Asahel in battle. Joab called for Abner to return to Hebron so he could speak to him privately and then he murdered him. David did not know of Joab's evil intent and lamented the death of Abner. David said of Abner, "Know ye not that there is a prince and a great man fallen this day in Israel." David said God would reward Joab for his deed.

---

1. Who came to Hebron to help David unite the kingdom?

2. Who killed Abner?

3. Why did he kill Abner?

4. Did David know of Joab's intent to kill?

5. David said, Abner was what two things?

Important Truths:

Unforgiveness will turn into bitterness.

Even great men can fall.

You will reap what you sow.

Wicked Men
II Samuel 4:9-11
(Study: II Samuel 4:1-12)

Ish-bosheth was the king of Israel, while David was the king of Judah. When Abner died, two brothers named Baanah and Rechab tried to transfer the kingdom to David thinking to benefit themselves. Ish-bosheth was murdered by these two brothers in his own house while he lay. When these two brothers brought the head of Ish-bosheth to David, thinking to get a reward, they received a death sentence instead. David told Baanah and Rechab that they were wicked men for slaying an innocent person upon his own bed, and in his own house. David commanded both of them to be hanged and killed.

---

1. Who was the king of Israel?

2. Who was the king of Judah?

3. Who killed Ish-bosheth?

4. Where did they kill him?

5. What did David have done to these two wicked brothers?

Important Truths:

Wrong actions are not justified by right outcomes.

Murder is wicked.

Never encourage family to do wrong.

David Made King of Israel
II Samuel 5:1-3
(Study: II Samuel 5:1-16)

David reigned in Hebron over Judah for seven years and six months and then all Israel came to him to ask him to be their king. They remembered that when Saul was king, David was the one who led them out and brought them in. They also knew that the Lord said concerning David, "Thou shalt feed my people Israel, and thou shalt be a captain over Israel." David was thirty years old when he began to reign, and he reigned forty years. David perceived that the Lord had established him as king over Israel, and that God had exalted his kingdom for His people Israel's sake.

---

1. How old was David when he began to reign?

2. How many years did David reign as king?

3. Who said David would be captain over Israel?

4. God exalted David's kingdom for whose sake?

5. What did Israel remember about David when Saul was king?

Important Truths:

Promotion comes from God.

God's timing is the best timing.

God places leadership for His people's sake.

David Enquires of the Lord
II Samuel 5:18-20
(Study: II Samuel 5:17-25)

The Philistines did not like it when they heard that David was anointed king over all Israel and they came up to get him. When David heard the Philistines were come up for him, he enquired of the Lord what he should do. God told him to go up, and that He would deliver them into David's hand. The Philistines were defeated that day, but decided to try again. David again enquired of the Lord what he should do, and the Lord told him to wait for a sound of going in the top of the mulberry trees, and then attack the Philistines. David did as God commanded and defeated the Philistines.

---

1. Who came up to get David?

2. To what valley did the Philistines come?

3. Who delivered the Philistines to David?

4. God told David to wait for a sound in what, before attacking the Philistines?

5. How many times did David enquire of the Lord and defeat the Philistines?

> **Important Truths:**
>
> Enquire of the Lord about everything.
>
> The enemy will try again and again.
>
> The Lord gives victory over the enemy.

The Error of Uzzah
II Samuel 6:6-8
(Study: II Samuel 6:1-11)

King David wanted to bring the ark of God to Jerusalem. He gathered 30,000 chosen men of Israel and put the ark on a new cart and brought it from Gibeah. David should have had the ark carried and not put on a cart. While transporting the ark on the cart, the oxen shook it and Uzzah put forth his hand and took hold of the ark to steady it. God was angry with Uzzah for his error in touching the ark and killed him. David was both afraid and displeased because the Lord had killed Uzzah for touching the ark. So David turned aside and placed the ark in the house of Obed-edom.

---

1. How did David transport the ark?

2. Where was David taking the ark?

3. Who touched the ark?

4. What did God do to Uzzah for his error of touching the ark?

5. Where did David place the ark of God after God killed Uzzah?

> **Important Truths:**
>
> Sins of ignorance still have consequences.
>
> People can be hurt when we do wrong.
>
> We should not do a right thing in the wrong way.

Michal Despises David
II Samuel 6:14-16
(Study: II Samuel 6:12-23)

David put the ark of God in the house of Obed-edom because of Uzzah being killed for touching the ark. David now goes again with all Israel to bring the ark to Jerusalem. Instead of putting it on a cart, they carry it like God had commanded. David showed his joy about bringing the ark to Jerusalem by sacrifices, shouting, dancing, and blowing the trumpet. Michal, David's wife, saw him rejoicing over the ark while watching from a window and despised him in her heart. When David returned home, she criticized him by saying he acted like a vain fellow. God punished Michal by not allowing her to have any more children.

1. Who was killed for touching the ark?

2. What did David do with all his might?

3. Who criticized David?

4. What did she say David acted like?

5. How did God punish her?

Important Truths:

It is a good thing to praise the Lord.

Viewers are often critical of doers.

God punishes a critical spirit.

God's Promise to David
II Samuel 7:14-16
(Study: II Samuel 7:1-17)

David had in his mind to build a house for the ark of God. When he told Nathan the prophet of his intention, he said, "do all that is in thine heart." However, that night God told Nathan to tell David he could not build Him a house, but that his son would. Along with this message, God made a promise to David that is known as the Davidic Covenant. That promise was that God would set up his seed after him, and that his kingdom and throne would be established forever. The significance of this promise is that Jesus, Who is in the lineage of David, will sit on the throne of David during the millennial reign of Christ and His kingdom will be forever.

---

1. What did David want to build?

2. Who did David ask about building a house?

3. What is God's promise to David called?

4. Who will sit on the throne of David next?

5. How long will His kingdom be established?

Important Truths:

God sometimes says no to His servants.

God always keeps His promises.

Jesus is King.

David's Prayer
II Samuel 7:27-29
(Study: II Samuel 7:18-29)

God told David he could not build a house for Him, but that his son Solomon would. He also promised David that his kingdom would be established forever. David responded with a prayer of thanksgiving to God. He said, "Who am I, O Lord GOD? And what is my house, that thou hast brought me hitherto? For thou hast confirmed to thyself thy people Israel to be a people unto thee for ever: and thou, Lord, art become their God." David magnified and praised the Lord for His promise to him and concerning Israel. David knew that it was God that brought him to being king and that he was not worthy of God's blessings.

---

1. Who would build a house for God?

2. What did God promise David?

3. How long will Israel be God's people?

4. Did David see himself worthy of God's blessings?

5. Of whom, did David say, "thy words be true"?

Important Truths:

None of us are worthy of God's kindnesses.

We should continually be thankful to God.

Israel will be God's people forever.

The Lord Preserves David
II Samuel 8:13-15
(Study: II Samuel 8:1-18)

Twice the Bible says, "And the LORD preserved David whithersoever he went." The word "preserved" means to be safe; avenge, defend, help, or rescue. In our story, God delivered David from the Philistines, Moabites, Syrians, Ammonites, Amalekites, and the Edomites. No one could stand up against David because the Lord stood with him. All these nations would come to fight against David with thousands in their armies, but every time David would defeat them. David was sure to give God the glory for all of these victories, as he would dedicate the silver and gold he took from these nations that he subdued.

---

1. What does the word preserve mean?

2. Who preserved David?

3. What did David execute in Israel?

4. From whom did God preserve David?

5. How did David glorify God for preserving Him?

Important Truths:

Safety comes from God.

The world would like to destroy the believer.

Give God the glory for your preservation.

David Is Kind to Mephibosheth
II Samuel 9:11-13
(Study: II Samuel 9:1-13)

David asked, Ziba, a servant of the former King Saul, "Is there not yet any of the house of Saul, that I may shew the kindness of God unto him?" Ziba told David that Jonathan had a son that was lame on his feet and his name was Mephibosheth. David sent for him and told him, "I will surely shew thee kindness for Jonathan thy father's sake." That day David made Mephibosheth as one of his own sons. He restored him all the land of Saul, and gave him Ziba and his sons to take care of the land, and had him eat bread at the king's table continually.

---

1. Who was a servant of Saul?

2. David showed kindness for whose sake?

3. What was the name of Jonathan's son?

4. Mephibosheth ate at the king's table as one of what?

5. What handicap did Mephibosheth have?

Important Truths:

God has shown us kindness for Jesus' sake.

All mankind has been affected by a fall.

God has made us as king's sons.

Wrong Thinking
II Samuel 10:1-3
(Study: II Samuel 10:1-19)

Nahash, the king of the Ammonites died and David sent men to his son to show kindness to him for the loss of his father. Unfortunately, the princes of the Ammonites convinced Hanun, Nahash's son, that David was only sending his men as spies and not as comforters. Hanun took David's servants and mistreated them and sent them away shamefully. Hanun knew that he offended David and hired Syrian soldiers to go to war with him against the children of Israel. However, they lost in battle and both the Syrians and the Ammonites fled from before Israel.

---

1. What Ammonite king died?

2. Who showed kindness to David?

3. Who was Nahash's son?

4. Who convinced Hanun that David was sending his servants as spies?

5. Who did the Ammonites hire to help them fight against Israel?

Important Truths:

Things are not always as they seem.

Don't be quick to jump to conclusions.

Quick decisions can have long lasting results.

The Fall before the Fall
II Samuel 11:2-4
(Study: II Samuel 11:1-5)

David was the one who killed the giant Goliath, he was the sweet psalmist of Israel, and the man after God's own heart. Yet, he also committed adultery with Bathsheba. David's sin of adultery would tarnish his great reputation for the rest of his life and beyond. However, David's sin did not start with adultery, but a series of sins led up to it. First, there was the sin of laziness for not going to battle when kings were supposed to go. Secondly, the sin of lust when he saw her from his rooftop and looked upon her. These sins led to committing adultery with Bathsheba. If he would have never been lazy or lusting, he would have never committed the sin of adultery.

---

1. What was one of the good things said of David?

2. With whom did David commit adultery?

3. What was David's first sin?

4. What was David's second sin?

5. What was David's third sin?

Important Truths:

Good Christians can commit great sins.

Little sins can turn into greater sins.

Some sins have greater consequences.

David Has Uriah Murdered
II Samuel 11:25-27
(Study: II Samuel 11:6-27)

After David committed adultery with Bathsheba, she became pregnant. David tried to cover up his sin by sending for Uriah from the battle to come be with his wife. When Uriah came, he would not go home, but slept at the door of the king's house. David even made Uriah drunk to get him to go home, but Uriah would not because the rest of David's servants were at battle in the open field. Since the pregnancy of Bathsheba could not be covered up, he had Uriah placed in the hottest part of battle where he would be killed. David then took Bathsheba as his wife, "But the thing that David had done displeased the LORD."

---

1. With whom did David commit adultery?

2. Who was Bathsheba's husband?

3. Why would Uriah not go home and be with his wife?

4. How did David have Uriah killed?

5. Who was displeased with David's actions?

Important Truths:

One sin will lead to another.

Sin displeases the Lord.

Servants can be more honorable than leadership.

David Repents of His Sin
II Samuel 12:12-14
(Study: II Samuel 12:1-14)

The Lord sent Nathan the prophet to David to reprove him for his sin of adultery with Bathsheba and for having her husband Uriah murdered by the children of Ammon. Nathan told David a story about a rich man who had herds of sheep, yet took the only sheep of a poor man to feed a traveler that came to him. When David heard this story, he became angry and said that this man should die and restore fourfold. Nathan said to David, "Thou art the man." David's response was "I have sinned against the LORD." God forgave David, but because of his sin, the enemies of the Lord would blaspheme and the child that was born to Bathsheba would die.

1. What man of God reproved David?

2. When David was confronted with his sin, what was his response?

3. Who would see the consequences of David's sin?

4. Who would die because of David's sin?

5. Who would blaspheme because of David's sin?

Important Truths:

God uses men of God to reprove us of sin.

Listening to reproof is wise.

God forgives those who will repent.

David's Child Dies

II Samuel 12:21-23

(Study: II Samuel 12:15-25)

David had committed adultery with Bathsheba and had her husband killed with the sword of the Ammonites. God was displeased with David for his sin. Though He forgave David, there were still consequences for his wrong doing. One of those consequences was the child that was born to Bathsheba would die. David fasted and prayed that God would spare the child, but seven days later the child died. David comforted Bathsheba over the loss of the child and God gave them another child that he named Solomon, and the Lord loved him.

---

1. How long did David fast and pray for the child?

2. What was one of the consequences for David's sin?

3. David knew that the child could not return to him, but that he could what?

4. What was the name of the second child born to Bathsheba?

5. How did God feel toward Solomon?

Important Truths:

God can forgive any sin.

Our families may suffer for our sins.

God is good to us even when we do not deserve it.

Human Loyalty
II Samuel 12:26-28
(Study: II Samuel 12:26-31)

Joab was the captain of David's army. He was very loyal to David, but not loyal to God. Twice he killed captains of armies when it was not a time of war. He was a great leader and a follower of David. When Joab went to war against the Ammonites, David stayed home. Joab defeated the Ammonites and was about to take the capital city, but would not go in because he knew the people would give the glory to him instead of King David. So Joab called for David and waited for him to come, before finishing the job of taking the capitol city. David came to Rabbah and fought against it, and took it, and received the honor for defeating the Ammonites.

---

1. Who was the captain of David's army?

2. What was the royal city of the Ammonites?

3. Joab was loyal to whom?

4. To whom was he not loyal?

5. Why would Joab not take the capital city?

Important Truths:

Our loyalty should always be to God first.

We should follow the man of God as he follows Christ.

Loyalty can be to something good or bad.

Amnon's Friend
II Samuel 13:3-5
(Study: II Samuel 13:1-22)

Amnon, David's son, had an affection for his sister Tamar, but knew he should not have her. Amnon had a friend named Jonadab who was a very subtil man. He advised Amnon to act like he was sick and to ask his father to send Tamar to make food that he might eat at her hand. David, not seeing the wicked plan, sent his daughter Tamar to Amnon. Amnon forced his sister to act immorally and then sent her away. This wicked act was done because of the advice and encouragement from an ungodly friend. Jonadab told Amnon what he wanted to hear, but not what he needed to hear.

---

1. Who was Amnon's father?

2. Who was Amnon's friend?

3. What kind of man was Jonadab?

4. For whom did Amnon have an affection?

5. Amnon tricked his father into sending Tamar to him by acting like he was what?

Important Truths:

Be careful whom your friends are.

A real friend does not encourage you to do wrong.

You can always find someone to agree with you.

Revenge of Absalom
II Samuel 13:27-29
(Study: II Samuel 13:23-39)

Absalom was the son of David and his mother was Maacah, the daughter of Talmai, king of Geshur. Amnon, his brother, forced his sister Tamar, and Absalom would get revenge for what he had done to his sister. Two years later, Absalom invited all the king's sons to a gathering, intending to kill Amnon. King David and his sons did not know of the anger or plot to kill Amnon. Absalom told his servants that when Amnon was merry with wine, they were to kill him. Absalom's servants did as he had commanded and all the king's sons fled and came to David. Absalom went to Talmai his grandfather, and David mourned for him every day.

1. Who was Absalom's grandfather?

2. Why did Absalom want to kill Amnon?

3. How many years later did Absalom get revenge?

4. Who did Absalom have kill Amnon?

5. For whom did David mourn everyday?

Important Truths:

Unforgiveness can lead to greater sins.

Getting revenge hurts everyone involved.

Time does not heal all wounds.

Wise Woman of Tekoah
II Samuel 14:2-4
(Study: II Samuel 14:1-20)

Joab, the captain of David's army, knew that the king's heart was toward Absalom, even though he had killed Amnon. David longed to go to Absalom, and he mourned over him every day. Joab asked a wise woman of Tekoah to go before the king and plead a fictitious case of her son being in trouble because of killing his brother. He hoped David would see it was alright to bring Absalom back home, in spite of what he did to Amnon. The woman of Tekoah told her story and then stated "the king doth not fetch home again his banished." David figured it was Joab that put these words in her mouth and told him to go and bring Absalom back again.

1. Why did Absalom leave David?

2. Did David want to go see Absalom?

3. Who put words into the woman's mouth that she spoke to David?

4. What did the woman of Tekoah feign herself to be?

5. Whom did David send to get Absalom?

Important Truths:

Children can break their parent's hearts.

Who is putting words in your mouth?

Forgiveness should come when there is repentance.

Partial Forgiveness
II Samuel 14:22-24
(Study: II Samuel 14:21-33)

After Absalom killed his brother Amnon, he fled to Gesher. David wanted to see him, but would not go after him. Joab encouraged David to let Absalom come home and David gave Joab permission to go get him. When Absalom returned to Jerusalem, David would not see him, but let him return to his own house. David had forgiven Absalom enough to bring him home, but not enough to actually see him. It was two full years before Absalom would be able to see his father face to face. Absalom requested through Joab to see the king and David granted his request.

1. Who encouraged David to bring Absalom home?

2. Where was Absalom before coming home?

3. David said to have Absalom return to his own house and not see whom?

4. How long would David not see Absalom?

5. Whom did Absalom ask to go before David to arrange a meeting?

Important Truths:

To forgive in part is to not forgive at all.

Never let unforgiveness linger.

Leadership must be forgiving.

Stolen Hearts

II Samuel 15:4-6
(Study: II Samuel 15:1-13)

Absalom, David's son wanted to be the king of Israel and replace his father. So Absalom would rise up early and wait by the gate for people to come to the king for judgment. When they came he would communicate with them of their dilemmas, compliment them of their matters, and tell them if he were king, he would do them justice. Over time Absalom stole the hearts of the men of Israel. His phony attention to their needs was for the purpose of taking over the kingdom. Absalom sent spies throughout Israel saying that "Absalom reigneth in Hebron," and the people increased continually with Absalom.

1. Who was David's son?

2. Whose hearts did Absalom steal?

3. Where would Absalom wait to steal their hearts?

4. From whom was Absalom stealing their hearts?

5. Why was Absalom stealing their hearts?

Important Truths:

Hearts can be stolen from authority.

We must be careful to whom we give our hearts.

People and things are not always as they seem.

David Flees Absalom
II Samuel 15:14-16
(Study: II Samuel 15:13-31)

In a time of trouble, David was able to see who his real friends were. Absalom had stolen the hearts of the people and was coming from Hebron to Jerusalem. David was warned of the conspiracy, and for the sake of those at Jerusalem, David left and went into the wilderness. Those who were loyal to David and left with him were his servants, namely the Cherethites, Pelethites, Gittites, 600 men of Gath, and Ittai. Those who wanted to go with David, but were asked to stay behind for his sake, were Zadok and Abiathar, the priests, and his friend Hushai. David left Jerusalem weeping, his head covered and he was barefoot.

---

1. From where was Absalom coming?

2. Where did David have to leave?

3. Where did David go?

4. What three people did David ask to stay back in Jerusalem?

5. Whom did David leave back to keep the house?

Important Truths:

During adversity, you find out who your friends are.

Sometimes you should walk away from a fight.

Those closest to you can hurt you the most.

David's Friend

II Samuel 15:35-37
(Study: II Samuel 15:32-37)

David is on the run from his son Absalom and has to leave the capital city of Jerusalem. When he leaves, the people most loyal to him go with him. One of those people was his friend Hushai. David asked Hushai to stay in Jerusalem and act as a servant to his son Absalom. David believed Hushai could help defeat the counsel of Ahithophel and could let David know what Absalom was planning to do. Hushai did what David asked, knowing he could lose his own life by doing so. Hushai was David's friend, and was willing to risk his life to help save his friend.

---

1. Who was David's friend?

2. David asked Hushai to fake being a servant to whom?

3. Whose counsel did David want to defeat?

4. Hushai risked what to help David?

5. To which two priests was Hushai to tell Absalom's plans?

Important Truths:

There is a friend that loveth at all times.

There is a friend that sticketh closer than a brother.

There is a friend that will lay down his life.

Shimei Curses David
II Samuel 16:11-13
(Study: II Samuel 16:5-14)

David's adversity not only brought to light his friends, but also his enemies. As David was fleeing Absalom, and headed to the wilderness, a man named Shimei cursed David as he went. Shimei was of the house of Saul. David's mighty men were on his right hand and on his left. Shimei cast stones at them, cursed them, and said, "come out, thou bloody man, and thou man of Belial." Abishai, one of David's soldiers wanted to kill him, but David would not let him. David said, "It may be that the LORD will look on mine affliction, and that the LORD will requite me good for his cursing this day."

---

1. To whom was Shimei related?

2. Who surrounded David?

3. What did Shimei throw at David and his servants?

4. Who wanted to kill Shimei for his actions?

5. Who did David say had bidden Shimei to curse him?

Important Truths:

There are those who will kick you when you're down.

Look for what the Lord is doing through others.

Do not dwell on what critics say about you.

Bitterness of Ahithophel
II Samuel 17:1-3
(Study: II Samuel 16:15-17:4)

Ahithophel was the counsellor of David, who was part of the conspiracy with Absalom to overthrow David. Ahithophel counselled Absalom on how to replace David as king. When David left Jerusalem, Ahithophel told Absalom that he would choose 12,000 men to go with him and that he would kill David. Ahithophel's ruthless plot to kill David was rooted in his bitterness for what David did when he committed adultery with Bathsheba, and killed her husband. Ahithophel was Bathsheba's grandfather (II Samuel 11:3; 23:34).

---

1. Whom was David's counsellor?

2. Whom did Ahithophel counsel to replace David?

3. How was Ahithophel related to Bathsheba?

4. What did Ahithophel want to do to David?

5. How many men did Ahithophel want to take with him when he went after David?

Important Truths:

Bitterness will ruin you.

Bitterness will cause you to ruin others.

Bitterness is the fruit of unforgiveness.

Ahithophel Hangs Himself
II Samuel 17:14-16
(Study: II Samuel 17:5-23)

Ahithophel wanted to kill David and told Absalom to give him 12,000 men and he would go after him. However, Absalom asked Hushai what he thought and he told him "the counsel that Ahithophel hath given is not good at this time." Hushai advised Absalom to go himself with all Israel to destroy David and all his men with him. Hushai told him this to save David's life from Ahithophel. God used the counsel of Hushai to defeat the counsel of Ahithophel and to bring evil upon Absalom. When Ahithophel saw his counsel was not followed, he went home and set his house in order and hung himself.

---

1. Whose counsel did Absalom say was better?

2. Who appointed the defeating of Ahithophel's counsel?

3. Hushai's counsel would bring evil upon whom?

4. Whom did Hushai tell to warn David of Absalom's plan?

5. What did Ahithophel do before he hung himself?

Important Truths:

The counsel of the Lord shall stand.

Killing yourself is never the right solution.

There is good and bad counsel.

Absalom Defeated
II Samuel 18:14-16
(Study: II Samuel 18:1-18)

Absalom went to battle against David's men in the woods of Ephraim. The day of the battle David told his captains, "Deal gently for my sake with the young man, even with Absalom." Twenty thousand people of Israel were slain before the servants of David that day. When Absalom was fleeing, he went under an oak tree and his hair got caught in the branches, and left him there hanging. Joab, one of David's captains came and took three darts "and thrust them through the heart of Absalom." Absalom died that day because of his rebellion, and all Israel fled to their tents.

---

1. David said to deal gently with whom?

2. How many Israelites were slain in the battle?

3. In what kind of tree did Absalom get his hair caught?

4. What did Joab thrust through the heart of Absalom?

5. Who blew a trumpet to end the battle?

Important Truths:

The love of a parent for his children is great.

A man should keep his hair cut short.

You should follow the King's wishes over yours.

Is Absalom Safe

II Samuel 18:31-33
(Study: II Samuel 18:19-33)

When Absalom was defeated in battle, Joab sent word back to David to let him know how the battle went. The first messenger that came to David was Ahimaaz, and the first question David asked was "Is the young man Absalom safe?" The second messenger that came was Cushi and David's first question again was, "Is the young man Absalom safe?" The answer was apparent that Israel was defeated and Absalom was killed. David's response was, "would God I had died for thee, O Absalom, my son, my son!" David loved Absalom so much that even though Absalom wanted to kill him, he still loved him anyway.

1. Who sent messengers to tell David about the battle?

2. Who was the first messenger that came to David?

3. Who was the second messenger that came to David?

4. What was David's question to the messengers?

5. Who did David wish would have died instead of Absalom?

Important Truths:

Love your enemies.

You are never safe when you go against God's man.

"Would God I had" is a bad way to live.

The King's Return
II Samuel 19:13-15
(Study: II Samuel 19:9-40)

After Absalom's defeat Israel requested for David to return as king. David made the journey back to Jerusalem and was met by three particular people. The first is Shimei who cursed and threw stones at David when he left. The second was Mephibosheth who was reproached by his servant Ziba as to why he did not go with David when he was fleeing from Absalom. The third was Barzillai who brought David food and supplies when he was in the wilderness. David showed kindness to all three. And all the people of Judah and half the people of Israel escorted King David back to his home.

---

1. Who did David promise would replace Joab as captain of the host?

2. Who was the first one to meet David on his return?

3. Who reproached Mephibosheth?

4. Who helped David in the wilderness?

5. What group of people escorted David back?

Important Truths:

One day, King Jesus will return for His own.

What we do now will be remembered by the King when He returns.

The believer will be rewarded for his works.

Joab Murders Amasa
II Samuel 20:8-10
(Study: II Samuel 20:1-12)

David came back to Jerusalem and commanded Amasa to assemble the men of Judah in three days to stop an insurrection by a man named Sheba. Amasa was the replacement for Joab as the captain of the host after returning from the battle with Absalom. Amasa took longer than the three days, and David sent Abishai to stop Sheba. Joab, Abishai's brother went also and met Amasa in the way. When Joab saw Amasa he said, "Art thou in health, my brother?" Amasa did not notice the sword that was in Joab's hand and when the two went to greet one another, Joab killed him.

1. Who replaced Joab as captain of the host?

2. Who was Amasa supposed to stop from leading a rebellion against David?

3. How many days did Amasa have to gather an army?

4. Because Amasa was late, whom did David send?

5. What did Joab ask Amasa before killing him?

Important Truths:

Being punctual can avoid a lot of problems.

Jealousy can be very cruel.

Hatred is usually covered by deceit.

Wise Woman of Abel
II Samuel 20:16-18
(Study: II Samuel 20:13-26)

King David sent his men to find Sheba who was trying to lead a revolt against him. Joab found him in the city of Abel and began to batter the wall to throw it down. A wise woman from inside the city called for Joab and asked why he was attacking the city. Joab said he had come for Sheba for going against the king. The wise woman told him that his head would be thrown to him over the wall. This "woman went unto all the people in her wisdom" to save the city and turn over Sheba to Joab. So they cut off Sheba's head and cast it over the wall. Joab immediately retired from the city and returned to Jerusalem.

---

1. Whom was Joab trying to find?

2. Where did he find him?

3. What did the wise woman tell Joab she would do?

4. Did the city do what the wise woman purposed?

5. Where did Joab go when he left Abel?

Important Truths:

Scorners cause trouble for those around them.

One wise person can save a host of people.

Cutting off scorners brings peace to everyone.

Saul's Forgotten Sin
II Samuel 21:1-3
(Study: II Samuel 21:1-14)

Saul was the first king of Israel. He lost the kingship because of his sin of entering into the priest's office and for not utterly destroying the Amalekites. However, Saul committed another sin that did not surface until after his death. Saul broke a covenant that Israel had made with the Gibeonites to not destroy them when they came into the land of Canaan. During David's reign, God sent a famine in punishment for Saul's disobedience. After three years of famine, David enquired of the Lord, and God told him it was for Saul killing the Gibeonites. Seven sons of Saul were hanged to make an atonement for the land.

1. What two sins caused Saul to cease from being king?

2. What sin of Saul came up after his death?

3. What was God's punishment for Saul killing the Gibeonites?

4. How many years did the famine last?

5. What was done to atone for the land?

Important Truths:

Some men's sins follow after them.

Sin's consequences will affect others.

What you do will affect your offspring.

David Waxed Faint
II Samuel 21:15-17
(Study: II Samuel 21:15-22)

David was a mighty king of Israel. He was the one who killed Goliath, the sweet psalmist of Israel, and a man after God's own heart. David went out to battle against the Philistines and waxed faint and was almost killed by a son of a giant named Ishbi-benob. One of David's mighty men named Abishai came to David's rescue and killed Ishbi-benob. David's men told him, "Thou shalt go no more out with us to battle, that thou quench not the light of Israel." David would no more go out and fight on the battlefield, but would lead Israel from the throne.

1. What was one of David's memorable traits?

2. Who tried to kill David in battle?

3. Who saved David's life?

4. Who told David he should not go to battle anymore?

5. If David died, whose light would be quenched?

Important Truths:

Christians can become faint in their warfare.

Christians should help keep brothers from becoming casualties.

Older Christians may have to change what they do for Christ.

David's Song
II Samuel 22:1-3
(Study: II Samuel 22:1-51)

David wrote this song of deliverance in the day that the Lord had delivered him out of the hand of all his enemies. David's enemies would have included Goliath, Saul, Doeg, Absalom, Ahithophel, the Amalekites, and all the other nations that came up against Israel. When David wrote this song he praised God for all that He had done for him. David said that God saved, took, drew, delivered, brought, delighted, recompensed, girded, gave, kept, avenged, and lifted him. Because of all that God had done for him he said, "Therefore I will give thanks unto thee, O LORD, among the heathen, and I will sing praises unto thy name."

---

1. In what day did David write this song?

2. Who were three of David's enemies?

3. What were three things that God did for David?

4. From what did David say God saved him?

5. What would David sing unto the Lord?

Important Truths:

It is God that delivers us from trouble.

We should praise the Lord for His goodness to us.

There will be enemies in the Christian life.

David's Last Words
II Samuel 23:1-3
(Study: II Samuel 23:1-7)

David was the second king of Israel and the man after God's own heart. He is called "the sweet Psalmist of Israel" because of the songs that he wrote that are recorded in the book of Psalms. David made it clear that it was the Spirit of God that spoke through him and put His word in his tongue. One of the last things that David would pass on, was what a man must be if he is to rule over men. There were two key things necessary for any ruler: he must be just, and he must rule in the fear of God. David did not think he lived up to both of these, but realized that God made with him an everlasting covenant.

---

1. Why was David called the sweet Psalmist of Israel?

2. Who spoke through David?

3. What two things must a ruler of men do?

4. What kind of covenant did God make with David?

5. Did David think he was a good example of a ruler of men?

Important Truths:

The Spirit of God can speak through a Christian.

There are requirements to leadership.

It is the mercy of God that one can lead.

David's Mighty Men
II Samuel 23:8-10
(Study: II Samuel 23:8-39)

David had thirty-seven mighty men. These men were loyal to him and risked their lives to protect him. Most of them are just mentioned by name, but five of them have something significant mentioned about them. Adino, slew 800 at one time by himself. Eleazar, smote the Philistines until his hand was weary, yet his hand clave to the sword. Shammah, defended a field of lentils and the Lord wrought a great victory. Abishai, lifted up his spear against three hundred and slew them. Benaiah, slew two lion-like men, as well as, a real lion. David set him over his guard.

---

1. How many mighty men did David have?

2. Which of David's mighty men slew 800?

3. Which of David's mighty men killed a lion?

4. Whose hand clave to the sword?

5. Who was set over David's guard?

Important Truths:

Loyal men are mighty men.

God does miraculous things with yielded people.

Strong leadership, attracts strong leadership.

David Numbers the People
II Samuel 24:2-4
(Study: II Samuel 24:1-25)

David decided that he wanted to number the people of Israel, even though it was not God's will. David sent Joab to number the people, and it took him nine months and twenty days. Joab came back and reported to David that there were 800,000 valiant men in Israel, and 500,000 in Judah. After David numbered the people, his heart smote him that he had sinned against the Lord. The prophet Gad came to David and told him he was to choose one of three punishments for numbering the people. David chose three days' pestilence and 70,000 Israelites died. David told the Lord that he had sinned and done wickedly.

1. Whom did David send to number the people?

2. How many Israelite men were there?

3. How many men of Judah were there?

4. Who was the prophet that reproved David?

5. How many died because of David's sin?

Important Truths:

Pride can cause a lot of damage.

Get advice before making a major decision.

Our decisions of life affect those around us.

I Will Be King
I Kings 1:5-7
(Study: I Kings 1:1-10)

King David was old and stricken in years. His son Adonijah, brother to Absalom, wanted to be king and began to enlist help for him to do so. Adonijah exalted himself and said "I will be king." He enlisted the help of Joab, captain of David's army, and Abiathar, the priest. It was God's will that Solomon be the next king after David. People who were closest to David knew this and did not follow after Adonijah, but waited for King David to say who was the next king. Adonijah called for most of his brethren and for all the men of Judah that were the king's servants to gain the support to make himself king. David, at first, did nothing to stop him.

1. Who was a very goodly man?

2. Who was Adonijah's brother?

3. Who did Adonijah get to help him?

4. Who did God say would be the next king?

5. Who at first, would not displease Adonijah?

Important Truths:

Making myself king is selfish and proud.

Promotion comes from the Lord.

Age can cloud a person's judgment.

Solomon Becomes King
I Kings 1:38-40
(Study: I Kings 1:11-40)

Adonijah gained a following as he tried to become the next king of Israel, but God had other plans. The prophet Nathan and Bathsheba came to King David and told him of Adonijah's intentions and asked him if that was the king's desire. King David assured them that Solomon would be the next king. David sent Zadok the priest, Nathan the prophet, and Benaiah the captain of the guard to take Solomon to Gihon and anoint him king in his stead. They anointed Solomon king and blew the trumpet and all the people said, "God save king Solomon." And Solomon came to Jerusalem and sat on his father's throne.

---

1. Who tried to become the next king of Israel?

2. What two people told David of Adonijah's intentions?

3. What three people did David send to anoint Solomon king?

4. Where did they anoint Solomon king?

5. What did all the people say when he was anointed?

Important Truths:

God's plans always supersede our own.

There is wisdom in listening to the man of God.

Only God can save the king.

David's Charge to Solomon
I Kings 2:1-3
(Study: I Kings 2:1-11)

David was old and about to die. He called for Solomon his son, the new king of Israel, and gave him his final charge. David told Solomon there were three things that he should make sure that he did. The first was to be strong, the second to show himself a man, and the third was to keep the charge of the Lord his God. In David's last words to Solomon, he also told him there were three people that he should reward according to their doings. The first was Joab, his captain of the host of Israel. The second was the sons of Barzillai, the man who helped David when he was running from Absalom, and the third was Shimei, who cursed David.

---

1. What was the first thing David charged Solomon?

2. What was the second thing David charged Solomon?

3. What was the third thing David charged Solomon?

4. Who helped David when he was running from Absalom?

5. Who had cursed David earlier in his life?

Important Truths:

A parent should leave a charge to their children.

There are principles and people to remember.

Every leader's reign will come to an end.

Respect for His Mother
I Kings 2:19-21
(Study: I Kings 1:12-25)

Solomon had just become king, and his mother Bathsheba came to speak with him. When he saw his mother, he stood up, bowed himself to her, and had a seat brought for her to sit at his right hand. Bathsheba was coming to make a request for Adonijah. He wanted to have Abishag for his wife. Abishag was a fair damsel that ministered unto his father King David. Solomon showed respect to his mother, but could not grant her request because Adonijah was up to no good and only wanted Abishag to try to get the kingdom for himself. King Solomon had Adonijah killed because there was wickedness in him.

---

1. Who was Solomon's mother?

2. How did Solomon show respect unto his mother?

3. For whom was Bathsheba making a request to Solomon?

4. Whom did Adonijah want for a wife?

5. Why did Solomon have Adonijah killed?

Important Truths:

Honor your father and mother.

Respect is not just a word, but an action.

Doing wrong is never right, no matter who asks you.

Unfinished Business
I Kings 2:26-28
(Study: I Kings 2:26-35)

When Solomon became king after David his father, there were a few people that deserved punishment, but David left it to Solomon to give them what they deserved. Two of those were friends of Adonijah, Joab, the captain of the host, and Abiathar the priest, who had tried to help him become the next king. Solomon banished Abiathar from Jerusalem and from being a priest. He spared his life because he was faithful during the reign of his father. Solomon had Joab executed because he killed Abner and Amasa without the consent of his father. Before he died, David told Solomon concerning Joab, "let not his hoar head go down to the grave in peace."

---

1. What was Abiathar's occupation?

2. What was Joab's occupation?

3. Who did Joab and Abiathar try to help?

4. Why did Solomon spare Abiathar's life?

5. Whom did David tell Solomon to not allow to die in peace?

Important Truths:

Be careful who your friends are.

God is a sure pay master.

Ending well is better than starting well.

Keep Your Promises
I Kings 2:36-38
(Study: I Kings 2:36-46)

Shimei cursed David when he was on the run from Absalom. When David returned from battle with Absalom, Shimei was one of the first to meet him to apologize for his actions. David pardoned his foolishness that day, but before he died, he told Solomon, "hold him not guiltless." When Solomon became king, he told Shimei to build him a house in Jerusalem and to never leave it, or he would surely die. Shimei promised the king that he would do his command. After three years, Shimei left Jerusalem to retrieve two of his servants in Gath. King Solomon had him executed for not keeping his promise of never leaving Jerusalem.

1. Who did Shimei curse with a grievous curse?

2. What place was Shimei to never leave?

3. Why did Shimei leave that place?

4. How many years later did Shimei break his promise?

5. What did Solomon do to Shimei for breaking his promise?

Important Truths:

Keep your promises, your life may depend on it.

Only repentance and obedience can fix past failures.

Time does not erase our commitments.

Prayer for Wisdom
I Kings 3:7-9
(Study: I Kings 3:1-15)

The Lord appeared to Solomon in a dream and said, "Ask what I shall give thee." Solomon recognized that God had showed great mercy to his father David, that He had placed him on the throne, and that he was not capable of doing the job on his own. Solomon asked God to give him an understanding heart, to be able to lead and judge the children of Israel. God was pleased with Solomon's answer and said, "Lo, I have given thee a wise and an understanding heart," so that there will be none like him before or after him. Along with wisdom, God gave Solomon riches and honor.

---

1. God spoke to Solomon in a what?

2. What question did God ask Solomon?

3. Solomon compared himself to a little what?

4. What kind of heart did Solomon ask God for?

5. What else did God give Solomon besides wisdom?

Important Truths:

Recognize your own capabilities, limits and God's abilities.

Ask God for wisdom and an understanding heart.

God knows our heart's desires.

Wisdom of Solomon
I Kings 3:25-27
(Study: I Kings 3:16-28)

One day, two harlots came to Solomon telling him of the death of a baby that each claimed belonged to her. Both of these harlots had a baby only three days apart, while living in the same house. The one accused the other of overlaying her baby, then taking her dead child during the night and exchanging it with the live child of the other mother. Solomon asked for a sword to divide the child that was left, but the real mother pleaded with the king to spare the child. The other woman said to go ahead and divide the child. Solomon knew from their responses which one was the real mother. All Israel heard of Solomon's judgment.

1. What kind of women came to king Solomon?

2. How many days apart were their babies born?

3. What did Solomon propose to do in order to find out to whom the living child belonged?

4. Who asked the king to spare the child?

5. Who heard of King Solomon's judgement?

Important Truths:

God gives true wisdom.

Even bad people deserve right judgment.

There is power in a mother's love.

Preparations for the Temple
I Kings 5:8-10
(Study: I Kings 5:1-18)

After Solomon became established as king, he wanted to begin building the temple. Solomon communicated with Hiram, king of Tyre, to help him with the materials for the project. Hiram respected David and was thrilled to be able to help his son build the temple. Solomon asked Hiram to help him with the timber and stones needed for building. Hiram agreed with Solomon to send timber of cedar and fir in exchange for food for his household. Solomon had over 180,000 Israelites working to provide stone and timber for the new temple. The stone would be used for the foundation of the house and the timber for its construction.

1. Who was the king of Tyre?

2. Whom did Hiram respect?

3. What kind of timber did Hiram send Solomon?

4. How many Israelites helped with the preparation for the temple?

5. What did Solomon give in exchange for the timber?

Important Truths:

Much can be accomplished with proper planning.

It is wise to use the help and skill of others.

Building something for God will cost you something.

Solomon Builds the Temple
I Kings 6:12-14
(Study: I Kings 6:1-7:51)

It took Solomon seven years to build the temple. He had the stones already made, so that there was not any tool of iron heard in the house while it was in construction. More important than the building of the temple, was Who it was built for. It would be called the House of God. God spoke to Solomon and told him that He would dwell among them and not forsake Israel if they would keep His commandments. Having a building for God to come to, was not nearly as important as having a people worth coming to. Solomon spared no expense, and built the house and finished it.

---

1. How long did it take to build the temple?

2. God told Solomon He would not forsake Israel if they did what?

3. What tools were heard while building?

4. Did Solomon spare expense in building it?

5. What is more important, buildings or people?

Important Truths:

Finish what you start.

Church buildings do not save lives, but what happens in them does.

Do things for God first class.

Prayer of Dedication
I Kings 8:22-24
(Study: I Kings 8:1-66)

After Solomon finished building the temple, he gathered together all the men of Israel to dedicate it to the Lord. They brought up the ark of the Lord unto the new temple. The only things inside the ark were the two tables of stone that God gave Moses at Horeb. When the priests came out of the holy place, the glory of the Lord filled the House of the Lord. Solomon kneeled before the altar in the presence of the congregation, raised his hands toward Heaven, and prayed a prayer of dedication of the new temple. Six times Solomon asked God that if Israel prayed from or toward the temple to God "then hear thou in heaven."

---

1. Who assembled to dedicate the temple?

2. What piece of furniture was put in the temple?

3. What was the only thing in the ark of the Lord?

4. What was Solomon's posture when praying?

5. What did Solomon say six times in his prayer to God?

Important Truths:

The house of God should be a house of prayer.

The house of God should be where the Bible is.

The house of God should be a dedicated place.

God Answers His Prayer
I Kings 9:3-5
(Study: I Kings 9:1-28)

Solomon prayed at the dedication of the temple for God to bless and answer the prayers of His people. God appeared to Solomon a second time and told him that if he would keep His commandments, that He would establish his kingdom. God also told Solomon, that if he turned from following Him and served other gods, then He would cut off Israel and destroy the house that he had built unto God. God's promise to Solomon came to pass, because as long as Solomon and the nation of Israel followed and obeyed God, He blessed them. If they went away and served false gods, God punished them.

---

1. Whose prayer was God answering?

2. How many times had God appeared to Solomon?

3. Where did God meet Solomon the second time?

4. What would God do, if Solomon kept God's commandments?

5. What would God do, if Solomon did not keep the commandments?

Important Truths:

God hears and answers prayer.

Blessings come with obedience!

God means what He says, and will do it!

Queen of Sheba
I Kings 10:7-9
(Study: I Kings 10:1-13)

The queen of Sheba heard of the fame of Solomon concerning the name of the Lord, and came to prove him with hard questions. Solomon answered all of her questions. When the queen of Sheba saw the house he built, the food he ate, the servants who attended him, and the house of the Lord, she was overwhelmed by what she saw. She told Solomon that it was true what she heard, but that the half had not been told her. The queen gave to Solomon gold, spices, and precious stones. Solomon in turn gave to her all her desire, whatsoever she asked before she returned to her own country.

1. The queen was from where?

2. How did the queen want to prove Solomon?

3. What caused Solomon's fame?

4. How many of the queen's questions did he answer?

5. What did Solomon give to the queen?

Important Truths:

We should be famous for spiritual things.

The world is looking for answers.

The half of heaven has not been told.

When Solomon Was Old
I Kings 11:4-6
(Study: I Kings 11:1-25)

Solomon was a great man. He was wiser than all men, because God gave him wisdom and understanding. He built a temple in honor to God, and he loved the Lord. However, when Solomon grew old, something changed. Solomon had 700 wives and 300 concubines who turned his heart away from the Lord. Solomon began to build high places for all of his wives' false gods, and God became angry with him. Twice, God warned Solomon that what he was doing was wrong, but he did not heed the warning. As a result, God told Solomon that He would take the kingdom away from him, and give it to his servant.

1. Solomon was wiser than whom?

2. How many wives did Solomon have?

3. What did Solomon do that made God angry?

4. How many times did God warn Solomon?

5. What punishment did Solomon suffer when he turned away from the Lord?

> **Important Truths:**
>
> A wife can be a strong influence.
>
> Things can slip as we get older.
>
> We had better heed God's warnings.

Israel Divided

I Kings 11:29-31
(Study: I Kings 11:26-43)

Saul, David, and Solomon were the first three kings of the nation of Israel. When he was old, Solomon began worshiping false gods, which angered the Lord. God warned Solomon, but he would not listen. God came to an industrious man named Jeroboam, through the prophet Ahijah, and told him that He would rend the kingdom of Israel. God told Jeroboam that he would be the king over ten of the tribes of Israel, but that one tribe would still belong to the house of David in Jerusalem. God told Jeroboam that if he would walk in His ways, then He would build Jeroboam a sure house, as He had built for David.

---

1. Who were the first three kings of Israel?

2. What did Solomon do that angered the Lord?

3. What prophet told Jeroboam he would be king?

4. Over how many tribes of Israel would Jeroboam reign?

5. What did Ahijah tear in pieces to illustrate the division of Israel?

Important Truths:

Promotion comes from the Lord.

God can give as well as take away.

God builds the house.

Counsel from the Old Men
I Kings 12:6-8
(Study: I Kings 12:1-24)

After Solomon died, his son Rehoboam was in line to be the next king of Israel. The Israelites came to Rehoboam and said, "Thy father made our yoke grievous," make it lighter, and we will serve you. Rehoboam asked for them to come back in three days for an answer. Rehoboam asked counsel from the old men, and they told Rehoboam that if he would serve them, they would be his servants forever. Rehoboam forsook the counsel of the old men and followed the counsel of those who grew up with him, who told him to make their yoke heavier. As a result, they refused to follow Rehoboam and the kingdom was divided.

1. Who had put a heavy yoke on Israel?

2. For how long did Rehoboam wait, before giving an answer to the children of Israel?

3. Who told Rehoboam to be a servant to the people?

4. Whose counsel did Rehoboam follow?

5. What happened because of Rehoboam's answer?

Important Truths:

Always get counsel for major decisions.

Those with age and experience are a good source of counsel.

If you are a servant, you will be served.

Jeroboam's New Worship
I Kings 12:26-28
(Study: I Kings 12:25-33)

When Rehoboam, the son of Solomon, became king, the kingdom was split. The northern kingdom of Israel followed Jeroboam and the southern kingdom followed Rehoboam. Jeroboam was concerned that all of his kingdom would go back to Jerusalem to worship and would return to following Rehoboam. He devised a plan to keep his kingdom worshiping in his own land. He made two golden calves, one he put in Dan and the other he put in Bethel. He copied everything of Israel's worship of God Jehovah and replaced it with a counterfeit.

---

1. Who was the king of the Northern Kingdom?

2. Who was the king of the Southern Kingdom?

3. What did Jeroboam make for Israel to worship?

4. Where did he put what he had made?

5. Where did Jeroboam not want his people to go?

Important Truths:

If God can make a leader, He can also make a follower.

Satan always counterfeits true worship

Worship is not about convenience.

Jeroboam Warned
I Kings 13:4-6
(Study: I Kings 13:1-10)

King Jeroboam led the children of Israel astray by placing golden calves and false altars in Dan and Bethel. God sent a prophet from Judah to speak against such wicked worship. The unnamed man of God prophesied that a man named Josiah would burn the bones of Jeroboam's false priests upon the altar that he had set up. Jeroboam, hearing this, stretched out his arm toward the man of God only to have God wither it, so that he could not pull it back in to him, and the altar was rent in two. Jeroboam asked the man of God to pray for him and have his hand made whole. He did pray and God healed Jeroboam. The king asked the man of God to come to his house and take a reward, but he refused.

1. From where did the man of God come?

2. What was the name of God's man?

3. Who would burn the bones of the false priests?

4. What happened to Jeroboam's arm?

5. Whom did Jeroboam ask to pray for him?

Important Truths:

Thou shalt have no other gods before me.

It is important to listen to the man of God.

God is merciful to the wicked.

Disobedient Man of God

I Kings 13:20-22
(Study: I Kings 13:11-34)

After the man of God from Judah delivered his message to Jeroboam against his false altar in Bethel, God commanded him to not tarry, but to go directly home. There was an old prophet in Bethel that heard from his sons what the man of God had said and done at Bethel. He went after him to bring him back to his house to give him food and refreshment. The old prophet lied to the man of God and told him an angel sent him to bring him back to his house. The man of God disobeyed God and went back, and for his disobedience God had a lion kill him. The old prophet brought his body to Judah and buried him.

---

1. Who lied to the man of God?

2. Where was the man of God from?

3. Who told the old prophet about the man of God?

4. What did God command the man of God to do?

5. What happened to the man of God for his disobedience to God?

Important Truths:

It is better to obey God, than man.

God's servants hold a greater responsibility.

Believing a lie, can kill you spiritually and physically.

The Sins of Jeroboam
I Kings 14:16-18
(Study: I Kings 14:1-20)

Jeroboam was the first king of the divided kingdom of Israel, and he reigned over ten tribes. Jeroboam did not want Israel going back to Jerusalem to worship God, so he set up two golden calves for Israel to worship and caused them to sin against God. Jeroboam's son fell sick and he sent his wife to Shiloh to ask the prophet Ahijah what would become of the child. Ahijah told Jeroboam's wife that because of his idolatry, God would take his son. God would bring evil upon the house of Jeroboam and take away those related to him. When Jeroboam's wife returned home, the child died, because of the sin of Jeroboam.

---

1. How did Jeroboam cause Israel to sin?

2. Who would die because of Jeroboam's sin?

3. Whom did Jeroboam send to ask the prophet what would become of his child?

4. What was the prophet's name?

5. Where was the prophet living?

Important Truths:

Sometimes God allows tragedy to get our attention.

When facing problems, go to the man of God.

Our sins influence our families.

Replacing Gold with Brass
I Kings 14:25-27
(Study: I Kings 14:21-31)

Israel as a nation, was divided into two kingdoms as a result of Solomon's heart being turned away from the Lord. Jeroboam led the Northern Kingdom and Rehoboam led the Southern Kingdom. It was not long into Rehoboam's reign that he led Judah to do evil in the sight of the Lord. They made images, built high places, allowed Sodomites in the land, and did other abominable things. God allowed Shishak, king of Egypt to come against Jerusalem and take away the treasures of the house of the Lord and the king's house. He even took away the 300 shields of gold that Solomon had made. Rehoboam replaced those golden shields with inferior shields of brass.

---

1. What are some of the sins of Rehoboam?

2. Who stole the golden shields?

3. How many golden shields were there?

4. Who made the golden shields?

5. What did Rehoboam use to replace the shields of gold?

Important Truths:

The world will steal what you have.

Spiritually, don't replace the best for less.

Sin will cause you to lose what you have.

Treason of Zimri
I Kings 16:18-20
(Study: I Kings 16:8-20)

After the nation of Israel was divided into two nations because of Solomon's sin, they had continual war with each other. Sometimes they had war within their own divided kingdom. Elah, the son of Baasha, ruled over Israel for two years in Tirzah. Zimri, was captain of half of his chariots and conspired against Elah and killed him. Zimri made himself king and immediately killed all of Elah's relatives and friends. Zimri's reign was short lived, because after seven days, Israel made Omri, who was a captain of the host, king. Omri came against Zimri with all Israel to Tirzah. When Zimri saw he was defeated, he went into the king's palace and burnt it over himself.

---

1. How long did Elah reign over Israel?

2. How long did Zimri reign over Israel?

3. Who defeated Zimri?

4. How did Zimri die?

5. The acts and treason of Zimri are written in what book?

Important Truths:

Disloyalty often leads to worse things.

You reap what you sow.

Promotion comes from God.

Evil King Ahab
I Kings 16:29-31
(Study: I Kings 16:23-34)

Omri was the worst king of Israel until his son Ahab was born. When Ahab became king, he did worse than his father and did more evil than the Israelite kings that preceded him. It was bad enough that Ahab continued in the sins of Jeroboam by worshipping the golden calves, but he added to it by serving Baal. Baal worship was instigated by the woman he married. Ahab married Jezebel, who was the daughter of Ethbaal, king of the Zidonians. Ahab did more to provoke God to anger than all the kings that were before him. In Samaria, the capital of the Northern kingdom of Israel, he built a house for Baal and set up an altar therein for people to come worship this false god.

---

1. Who was Ahab's father?

2. Who was Ahab's wife?

3. Who was the father of Ahab's wife?

4. Where was the capital of the Northern Kingdom?

5. For what false god did Ahab build a house?

Important Truths:

Children learn by example.

Marriage can make you better or worse.

Bad leadership can corrupt any people.

Widow of Zarephath
I Kings 17:12-14
(Study: I Kings 17:1-16)

Elijah the prophet, told Ahab, the king of Israel, that there would be no rain according to his word. Then God sent Elijah to the brook Cherith and ravens came and fed him morning and evening until the brook dried up. Then the Lord sent Elijah to Zarephath so that a widow woman could sustain him. When Elijah asked her for a morsel of bread, she said she only had a handful of meal in a barrel and a little oil in a cruse. Elijah said that she should make for him first and that the Lord would not allow the barrel of meal to waste or the cruse of oil to fail until God sent rain upon the earth. She followed his instructions, and Elijah and her house ate many days.

---

1. Who did Elijah tell that it would not rain?

2. Where did God send Elijah to be fed by ravens?

3. How often did the ravens feed him?

4. For whom was the widow woman gathering sticks, to make a last meal?

5. How long did the widow's meal and oil last?

Important Truths:

The Lord takes care of His people.

God can use unusual means to take care of us.

Put God first, and He will take care of you.

The Widow's Son
I Kings 17:20-22
(Study: I Kings 17:17-24)

Elijah performed the miracle of the barrel of meal and the cruse of oil not going empty during famine, for the widow of Zarephath. During this time, the widow's son fell sick and died. She carried her son to Elijah and asked him why this happened. Elijah took the lifeless boy and cried unto the Lord that He would restore the life of the child. Three times Elijah cried unto the Lord, and God answered his prayer and restored the child's life. When Elijah brought the child down and returned him to the widow woman, she said, "Now by this I know that thou art a man of God, and that the word of the LORD in thy mouth is truth."

---

1. What miracle did Elijah do for the widow first?

2. Who died in the story?

3. How many times did Elijah pray for the child's life?

4. Whose voice did God hear?

5. What two things did the widow of Zarephath now know after receiving her child alive again?

Important Truths:

God can perform any miracle.

Problems should be taken to the man of God.

Some answers to prayer require persistence.

A Secret Believer
I Kings 18:3-5
(Study: I Kings 18:1-16)

Obadiah was the governor of King Ahab's house. Ahab was the wicked king of Israel who had Jezebel as his wife. Obadiah feared the Lord greatly from his youth, but could not make it known. Jezebel was a Baal worshipper and slew the prophets of God. Obadiah, as a believer in God, protected the prophets of God, by hiding them in a cave, and he fed them with bread and water. After three years of famine and no rain, Ahab sent Obadiah out to find water that they might save some of the animals alive. While Obadiah was searching for water, he crossed paths with Elijah. Elijah told Obadiah to tell Ahab that he would meet with him that day!

1. Who was the governor of Ahab's house?

2. Who killed the prophets of God?

3. What did Obadiah do from his youth?

4. How long had there been no rain?

5. Who did Elijah tell Obadiah that he would meet with that day?

Important Truths:

Even a secret believer can do something for God.

God has His servants in positions of power.

You should fear God as a youth!

Two Opinions
I Kings 18:20-22
(Study: I Kings 18:17-24)

Ahab and Elijah finally meet after more than three years of no rain, and the first words out of Ahab's mouth were "Art thou he that troubleth Israel?" Elijah told Ahab that he was the one that had troubled Israel because he had forsaken the commandments of God and followed Baalim. Ahab gathered the children of Israel to Mount Carmel, and Elijah asked them "How long halt ye between two opinions?" Then Elijah offered a challenge to the false prophets of Baal. He suggested that they each set up an altar with a sacrifice. Then the prophets could call upon Baal and he would call upon the Lord. The God that answered by fire would be God. The people agreed and said, "It is well spoken."

---

1. How long had there been no rain?

2. What did Ahab say to Elijah when they first met?

3. Where did Ahab gather the people to meet Elijah?

4. Whom did Elijah challenge to prove who was God?

5. Elijah said that the God that answered by what should be God?

Important Truths:

There will be two opinions: right and wrong.

One will always have to choose between the two.

God is always the right choice!

Fire from Heaven
I Kings 18:36-38
(Study: I Kings 18:22-41)

Elijah went to Mount Carmel for a contest with the 450 false prophets of Baal. The challenge would be whose God would send fire down from Heaven to consume their animal sacrifice. Would it be Baal or the Lord God? The false prophets of Baal called on their god from morning until evening, with no fire or answer. Elijah called the people together and had them dig a trench around the altar, and then filled the trench with 12 barrels of water. Elijah only prayed 63 words, and God sent fire down from heaven consuming the sacrifice and all the water he had put on it. When the people saw it, they said, "the LORD, He is the God; the LORD He is the God."

---

1. Where did Elijah call fire down from Heaven?

2. How many false prophets were there?

3. How many barrels of water were put on Elijah's altar?

4. How many words did Elijah pray for fire to fall?

5. What did the people say when the fire fell?

Important Truths:

There is only one true God.

There are more false worshippers than true ones.

God can do the impossible!

God Sends Rain
I Kings 18:42-44
(Study: I Kings 18:42-46)

After the contest on Mount Carmel, the 450 false prophets of Baal were killed. Elijah began to pray for rain. The whole reason for Ahab coming with Israel to meet with Elijah was because of a three-year famine with no rain. Elijah went to the top of Mount Carmel with his servant and asked God to send the rain. Seven times Elijah told his servant to go and look toward the sea to see if there was any rain coming. The last time the servant said he saw a little cloud, like a man's hand. Elijah knew it was God's hand of rain. The heaven became black with clouds and wind, and there was a great rain.

---

1. What happened to the 450 false prophets of Baal?

2. How long was the famine in Israel?

3. Where did Elijah go to pray for rain?

4. How many times did Elijah's servant go look for rain?

5. What did the servant see arise out of the sea?

Important Truths:

Prayer can move the hand of God.

Sometimes we need to pray until we get an answer.

The prayer of God's man helped an entire nation.

Running from Jezebel
I Kings 19:2-4
(Study: I Kings 19:1-7)

Elijah had just seen the miracles of God: fire falling from Heaven, 450 false prophets being slain, and God sending rain after a three-year famine. Jezebel, Ahab's wife, did not take kindly to Elijah slaying the 450 false prophets of Baal, and sent a messenger to tell him that she would have him killed by the next day. Elijah ran for his life into the wilderness and asked for God to take away his life. As Elijah lay under a juniper tree, an angel came to him and had him eat. After he rested, the angel came again and fed him and said, "Arise and eat; because the journey is too great for thee."

---

1. What miracles did Elijah get to see?

2. Who wanted to kill Elijah?

3. Where did Elijah run after being threatened?

4. What was Elijah lying under when the angel came to feed him?

5. What did the angel say was too great for Elijah?

> **Important Truths:**
>
> Words can affect anyone for good or bad.
>
> God can help us with our journey of life.
>
> Discouragement can come after great victory.

The Still Small Voice
I Kings 19:10-12
(Study: I Kings 19:8-18)

Elijah was running from Jezebel's threats to kill him and an angel fed him before he took his journey to Mount Horeb to meet with God. For forty days, Elijah fasted and lodged in a cave in Mount Horeb. The Lord showed His presence in a wind, an earthquake, and a fire. When Elijah heard a still small voice, he knew it was God, and wrapped his face in his mantle, and went and stood in the entering of the cave. God asked Elijah, "What doest thou here, Elijah?" Elijah told God that he was the only one left and that they sought to kill him too. God told Elijah that He had 7,000 in Israel that still had not bowed a knee to Baal.

---

1. On what mountain did Elijah meet God?

2. How long did Elijah fast to hear from God?

3. How many people did not bow to Baal?

4. What did Elijah do when he heard the still small voice?

5. Who sought to kill Elijah?

Important Truths:

God has a faithful remnant that are unknown to us.

Fasting and prayer will help you hear God's voice.

Our great God sometimes speaks in a small voice.

The Call of Elisha
I Kings 19:19-21
(Study: I Kings 19:15-21)

When Elijah was on Mount Horeb, God told him to anoint Elisha to be the prophet in his place. When Elijah came down from the mountain, he found Elisha plowing in the field. Elijah simply went up to him and cast his mantle upon him. Elisha knew that was his calling of God to follow Elijah and prepare to be God's man for Israel. Elisha left nothing to go back to, as he sacrificed the oxen he was plowing with and said goodbye to his parents. "Then he arose, and went after Elijah, and ministered unto him."

---

1. Where was Elijah when God told him that Elisha would be the next prophet?

2. What did Elijah do to show Elisha God was calling him to be the next prophet?

3. What did Elisha sacrifice before following Elijah?

4. What did Elisha do after following Elijah?

5. Who did Elisha kiss goodbye?

Important Truths:

God chooses people to serve Him who are already doing something.

Replacements are necessary in God's service.

God wants His children to be servants.

Victory by the Young Men
I Kings 20:19-21
(Study: I Kings 20:1-21)

Ben-hadad, king of Syria, gathered his host and 32 kings with him and went up and besieged Samaria. Ahab was the king of Israel at Samaria. God sent a prophet to Ahab and told him that He would deliver this great host into his hand, that he might know that He was God. Ahab asked God how and who would lead the battle. God told Ahab that the young men of the princes of the provinces would be his fighters and that He would order the battle. Two hundred thirty-two young men went out to fight against Ben-hadad's great host, and defeated them. Israel slew the Syrians with a great slaughter, but Ben-hadad escaped on horseback.

---

1. Who was the king of Syria?

2. Who was the king of Israel?

3. How many young men were there?

4. Who told Ahab that Syria would be defeated?

5. Who followed the young men into battle?

> **Important Truths:**
>
> It is alright to be outnumbered as long as you have God.
>
> God uses young people to do the impossible.
>
> God can use a wicked leader to bring Him glory.

Syrians Try Again
I Kings 20:28-30
(Study: I Kings 20:22-30)

Ben-hadad, king of Syria, came up against Israel and lost, but did not give up. At the return of the year he gathered his army again to fight against Israel. The Israelites were like two little flocks of sheep in comparison to the Syrians that filled the country. God sent a man of God to tell Ahab, the king of Israel, that He would deliver the Syrians into his hand, that he might know that the Lord was God. After seven days, the battle was joined, and Israel slew 100,000 footmen. The 27,000 that were left, fled into a city where God allowed a wall to fall and kill them.

1. Where was Ben-hadad the king?

2. Who did God send to talk to King Ahab?

3. How many Syrians died in the battle?

4. How many Syrians died by a wall falling on them?

5. God told Ahab He would deliver this great multitude into his hand that he might know what?

Important Truths:

You cannot fight against God and win.

God does miracles that we might know that He is God.

It is not how many are on your side but whose side you are on.

Sparing Ben-Hadad
I Kings 20:41-43
(Study: I Kings 20:31-43)

Ben-hadad, king of Syria, came up twice to destroy Israel and lost. When Ben-hadad was taken in battle, Ahab, the king of Israel, spared his life, made a covenant with him, and sent him away. God sent a prophet to Ahab. The prophet disguised himself and waited for the king. The prophet told Ahab that he was a soldier and was supposed to keep a prisoner, and that if he lost him, his life was supposed to be taken. When the king heard his story, he told him "So shall thy judgment be." The prophet took off his disguise and told Ahab that because he let Ben-hadad go, whom God appointed to destruction, that his life and people would be lost.

1. How many times did Syria come against Israel?

2. Whose life did Ahab spare in battle?

3. Who did God send to reprove Ahab?

4. What did God appoint for Ben-hadad?

5. How did Ahab go up to his house after hearing the reproof from the prophet?

Important Truths:

You had better do what God says to do.

Don't be too quick to judge someone else.

Helping those whom God is against will get you in trouble.

Naboth's Vineyard
I Kings 21:2-4
(Study: I Kings 21:1-16)

Ahab saw Naboth's vineyard and wanted to have it. He offered to give Naboth a better vineyard, or pay him money for it, but Naboth would not give away the inheritance of his fathers. Ahab came home displeased and would not eat. When Jezebel his wife inquired, Ahab explained that Naboth would not sell him his vineyard. Jezebel sent to the elders of Naboth's city to set up a special day in which they would honor Naboth. Then they plotted to have two false witnesses say that Naboth blasphemed God and the king, and to have him taken out and stoned to death. This they did, and Jezebel told Ahab that he could take possession of Naboth's vineyard because he was dead.

---

1. Why would Naboth not sell his vineyard?

2. Who orchestrated Naboth's murder?

3. Of what did the false witnesses accuse Naboth?

4. How was Naboth killed?

5. Who told Ahab he could have Naboth's vineyard?

Important Truths:

Wicked men do wicked things.

You cannot have everything you want.

Some things are not for sale.

Ahab's Doom
I Kings 21:24-26
(Study: I Kings 21:17-29)

After Jezebel organized the death of Naboth, Ahab went down to take possession of Naboth's vineyard. God sent Elijah to meet Ahab there and pronounce his doom because of the evil he had worked in the sight of the Lord. When Ahab saw Elijah, he said, "Hast thou found me, O mine enemy?" God told Ahab that He would bring evil upon him and destroy his posterity. When Ahab heard these words he rent his clothes, put on sackcloth, fasted, and went softly. When God saw how Ahab humbled himself, He said He would not bring the evil in Ahab's days, but in his son's days.

---

1. Who stirred up Ahab to do wickedly?

2. Where did Elijah meet Ahab?

3. What did Ahab call Elijah?

4. What was Ahab's doom?

5. What did Ahab do that caused God to lessen his punishment?

Important Truths:

A wife can stir up her husband for good or bad.

God can show mercy to the worst of sinners.

Be sure your sin will find you out.

Ahab's Lying Prophets
I Kings 22:6-8
(Study: I Kings 22:1-12)

Ahab wanted to take back Ramoth in Gilead from the Syrians, so he asked Jehoshaphat, king of Judah, to help him. Jehoshaphat asked Ahab to enquire of the Lord to see if they should. Ahab gathered his 400 false prophets together to show Jehoshaphat that they should go up against Syria. It must have not been too convincing because Jehoshaphat asked if there were any other prophets they could enquire from. Ahab said there was one named Micaiah, but that he hated him because he never prophesied good concerning him, but evil. While Ahab called for Micaiah to come, his false prophets lied saying, "Thus saith the LORD," thou shalt push the Syrians, until thou have consumed them.

1. Who was Ahab trying to get to go to war with him?

2. What city did Ahab want to take back?

3. How many false prophets did Ahab have?

4. How did Ahab feel about Micaiah?

5. What did Micaiah prophesy concerning Ahab?

Important Truths:

Backsliders can get you into trouble.

You can always find someone to agree with wrong.

You should never hate the man of God.

Micaiah, God's Man
I Kings 22:26-28
(Study: I Kings 22:13-28)

Ahab, king of Israel and Jehoshaphat, king of Judah were waiting to hear what Micaiah the prophet was going to say about going to battle at Ramoth-gilead. When Micaiah arrived, he told them that if they go to battle, they will lose and that Ahab's 400 prophets have a lying spirit in their mouths. Zedekiah, one of the false prophets hit Micaiah on the cheek and said it was the spirit that told him to do so. Ahab did not like what Micaiah had to say and had him arrested and put in prison for what he had prophesied. Ahab and Jehoshaphat followed the advice of the 400 hundred false prophets instead of Micaiah, the true man of God.

1. Who was the king of Israel?

2. Who was the king of Judah?

3. Who had a lying spirit in their mouths?

4. Who smote Micaiah on the cheek?

5. What did Ahab do to Micaiah because he told him the truth?

Important Truths:

Sometimes people do not want to hear the truth.

We should do right regardless of the outcome.

Real men of God tell the truth.

God Drops the Arrow
I Kings 22:34-36
(Study: I Kings 22:29-40)

Ahab, the king of Israel, and Jehoshaphat, king of Judah, went up to Ramoth-gilead to battle against the king of Syria. Ahab disguised himself so that the enemy would not know he was the king. However, God had a certain man draw his bow and shoot an arrow into the air. That arrow dropped right upon Ahab and mortally wounded him. That evening Ahab died and they brought his body back to be buried in Samaria. All Israel and Judah returned to their own cities. As they washed Ahab's chariot in the pool of Samaria, the prophecy that "the place where dogs licked the blood of Naboth shall dogs lick thy blood" came to pass.

1. Where was the battle between Israel and Syria?

2. Why did Ahab disguise himself?

3. The arrow that killed Ahab smote him where?

4. Where was Ahab buried?

5. What prophecy came true about Ahab?

Important Truths:

You cannot hide from God.

The safest place is in the center of God's will.

God often uses unnamed people in our lives.

If I Be a Man of God
II Kings 1:10-12
(Study: II Kings 1:1-18)

Ahaziah, the son of Ahab, fell through a lattice and was sick. He sent messengers to go inquire from Baal-zebub the god of Ekron, whether or not he would recover. The prophet Elijah met the messengers and told them that the king would surely die. When the king heard what Elijah had said, he sent a captain and fifty soldiers to bring Elijah to him. They demanded that he come, but Elijah responded that if he was a man of God, then let fire fall from Heaven upon them. Ahaziah sent another captain with fifty to bring Elijah, and the same thing happened to them. The third time, the captain that came, pleaded for his life. Elijah went with them and told Ahaziah that he would surely die.

1. Who was Ahaziah's father?

2. Ahaziah sent to inquire with what false god?

3. Who told Ahaziah he would surely die?

4. How many captains were sent to bring Elijah?

5. How many men died by fire falling from heaven?

Important Truths:

Men of God take their orders from God.

Man cannot make demands with God.

The life of man is in the hands of God.

Elisha Gets Double
II Kings 2:9-11
(Study: II Kings 2:1-15)

Elijah was the man of God that called fire down from Heaven, and he was about to be translated to Heaven alive in a whirlwind. Elisha was his servant and wanted that same spirit and power of God that Elijah had. Before God took him to Heaven, Elijah asked Elisha what he could do for him. Elisha responded, "let a double portion of thy spirit be upon me." Elijah told him he would get his request as long as Elisha saw him when he was taken to Heaven. Shortly after, a chariot of fire appeared and parted them both asunder and Elijah went up to Heaven in a whirlwind. Elisha saw Elijah taken up to Heaven and received a double portion of the spirit of Elijah.

1. Who called fire down from Heaven?

2. Who did God take to Heaven in a whirlwind?

3. What did Elisha request of Elijah?

4. What did Elisha have to do to get what he requested?

5. What parted Elijah and Elisha while they walked?

Important Truths:

Keep a close relationship with the man of God.

Ask God for the impossible.

Have a desire to do more than your predecessors.

Be Careful What You Say
II Kings 2:23-25
(Study: II Kings 2:16-25)

Elisha was the prophet who replaced Elijah and had received a double portion of his spirit. When Elisha came to the town of Bethel, he was met by little children who mocked him by saying, "Go up, thou bald head; go up, thou bald head." Elisha turned around and cursed them in the name of the Lord. God sent two she bears out of the woods to teach them a lesson about mocking the man of God. Forty-two children were torn by those bears for disrespect to God's man. The word Bethel means house of God, yet the children that came out of such a city did not know the importance of God's messenger.

1. What town was Elisha in when he was mocked?

2. What did the children mockingly say?

3. What did God send to punish those children?

4. How many children were torn by she bears?

5. Where did Elisha go after he left Bethel?

Important Truths:

We will be judged for what we say.

You should not show disrespect to God's man.

Even the animal kingdom obeys God.

Reputation of a Servant
II Kings 3:10-12
(Study: II Kings 3:1-12)

The kings of Judah, Israel, and Edom came together to go to battle against the king of Moab. Their travel to Moab took seven days through a wilderness with no water for them or their cattle. Jehoshaphat, the king of Judah, asked, "Is there a prophet that we can inquire of the Lord by?" A servant of the king of Israel answered his question by saying, "Here is Elisha the son of Shaphat, which poured water on the hands of Elijah." Years after Elijah had been translated to heaven, Elisha was known for being a servant to the man of God. Jehoshaphat knew by Elisha's association with Elijah that "the word of the LORD is with him."

---

1. Which three kings came to together to go to war?

2. Against whom were they going to war?

3. How many days did they travel to go to battle?

4. To what prophet did the three kings go for advice?

5. Elisha was known for what?

Important Truths:

The answer to every problem is God.

A good reputation is that of being a servant.

Our associations tell much about us.

Valley Full of Ditches
II Kings 3:16-18
(Study: II Kings 3:13-27)

The kings of Edom, Israel, and Judah joined forces to come up against the Moabites. Seven days into their journey to battle, they found themselves with no water. These three kings came to the prophet Elisha and asked him to inquire of God for them, that they might get water for their soldiers and animals. Elisha told them to dig ditches and that God would fill them with water. They did as Elisha said and dug ditches in the valley and the next morning God filled the country with water. Not only did God give them water, but he also gave them the victory over the Moabites.

1. Which kings came up against the Moabites?

2. How many days journey had they come?

3. What did Elisha tell the kings to do?

4. God filled the country with what?

5. Did they see wind and rain when God sent the water?

> **Important Truths:**
>
> The man of God can get answers from God.
>
> If we do our part, God will do His.
>
> Some things seem impossible, but God is able.

The Creditor Is Come
II Kings 4:3-5
(Study: II Kings 4:1-7)

There was a certain widow woman, whose husband feared the Lord and he was one of the sons of the prophets. When her husband died, they owed a debt. The creditor came and demanded payment or her two sons were to become his bondmen to work off the debt. This widow woman came to Elisha the prophet for help. He asked what she had in her house, and she said only a pot of oil. He told her to go and borrow empty vessels and then pour out the oil she had into them. The oil miraculously filled all the vessels. He then told her to sell the oil and pay her debt. She and her children would then live off of the rest of the money.

1. What do we know about the widow's husband?

2. How many sons did the widow have?

3. Who did the widow go to for help?

4. What was the only thing of value that the widow had in the house?

5. What was the widow told to borrow?

Important Truths:

God can use what we have to meet our needs.

It is wise to pay your debts so others will not have to.

Pay your debts.

The Great Woman of Shunem
II Kings 4:8-10
(Study: II Kings 4:8-17)

The prophet Elisha passed by a city called Shunem on a regular basis. There was a woman there that would urge Elisha to stop at her house and eat whenever he passed by. The woman is not named, but was called "a great woman." Over time she recognized that Elisha was a "holy man of God" and asked her husband to make a chamber where Elisha could rest whenever he passed by. They built the chamber on the wall and put inside of it a bed, table, stool, and candlestick. Elisha wanted to reward her for her kindness, but she would require nothing. Elisha knew there was one thing she wanted and that was to have a child. Elisha told her she would have a son, and she did.

1. What was the woman of Shunem called?

2. What did she recognize Elisha to be?

3. What did she and her husband make for Elisha?

4. What did she put in the chamber for Elisha?

5. How did Elisha reward her for her kindness?

Important Truths:

Take care of the man of God.

God gives back more than we give out.

Great people are often unnamed or unnoticed.

Son Restored to Life
II Kings 4:33-35
(Study: II Kings 4:18-37)

The great woman of Shunem was rewarded for her kindness to Elisha by having a son. She and her husband had made a prophet's chamber for the man of God to stay in whenever he passed by. When the child was grown he had become ill with a terrible headache and died. The Shunammite woman put her child on the bed in Elisha's chamber and then went to Mount Carmel to find Elisha. When she came to Elisha she fell at his feet and would not let him go unless he came with her. Elisha came to the house and found the child dead in his room. He shut the door with him and the child and began to pray. God answered his prayer and brought the child back to life and returned him to his mother.

---

1. What did the Shunammite woman do for Elisha?

2. What did Elisha do for the Shunammite woman?

3. Where did the Shunammite woman find Elisha?

4. Where did the Shunammite put her dead son?

5. Did God answer Elisha's prayer immediately?

> **Important Truths:**
>
> God allows tragedy to test our faith.
>
> Fervent prayer can change things.
>
> Great miracles are a result of great faith.

Death in the Pot
II Kings 4:39-41
(Study: II Kings 4:38-41)

Elisha the prophet came to Gilgal, and there was a famine in the land. The sons of the prophets came and sat before Elisha, and Elisha told his servant to boil some soup for them. One of them went out and instead of gathering herbs, he gathered wild gourds that were poisonous. Unknown to everyone, these gourds caused the entire pot of soup to be poisonous. While they were eating the soup someone cried out to Elisha, "there is death in the pot." Elisha told them to put some meal in the pot and God miraculously healed the pot of its poison and they were able to eat of it with no harm.

---

1. Elisha came to what city?

2. What was going on in the land?

3. Who sat before Elisha?

4. What was put into the soup that made it poisonous?

5. What was put into the soup to fix it?

> **Important Truths:**
>
> One bad thing can ruin the whole.
>
> Things that look good are not always good.
>
> Some things need fixed, not thrown away.

Naaman the Leper
II Kings 5:13-15
(Study: II Kings 5:1-19)

Naaman was the captain of the Syrian army, but he had the disease of leprosy. One day a little maid, who was taken captive from Israel, said to Naaman's wife, "Would God my lord were with the prophet in Samaria, for he would recover him of his leprosy." Naaman went to the prophet Elisha to be healed and was expecting Elisha to say some words and heal him. Instead, the prophet told him to go dip himself seven times in the river Jordan. Naaman did not like this remedy, but went and did it anyway. After dipping himself seven times, he came up healed of his leprosy. Naaman returned to Elisha to praise God and show his gratefulness.

---

1. Who was the captain of the Syrian army?

2. What deadly disease did he have?

3. What prophet healed him of his disease?

4. What did he tell Naaman to do to be healed?

5. What did Naaman know after he was healed?

Important Truths:

We should be grateful for God's miracles.

A little maid can do a lot of good.

For God to work, we must do it His way.

Gehazi's Greed
II Kings 5:25-27
(Study: II Kings 5:20-27)

God used Elisha to heal Naaman of his leprosy. Gehazi was Elisha's servant and saw the miracle, and saw how Elisha refused to be recompensed monetarily for healing Naaman. Gehazi went after Naaman and lied to him by saying that his master had sent him for money and garments for two young men that had come to him. Naaman was more than willing to give to Elisha after being healed of his leprosy, and gave Gehazi "two talents of silver in two bags, with two changes of garments." When Gehazi returned to Elisha he lied again concerning where he had been. Elisha told Gehazi that for what he had done, he and his seed would have Naaman's leprosy.

1. Who did Elisha heal of leprosy?

2. Who was Elisha's servant?

3. What did Naaman give to Gehazi?

4. What lie did Gehazi tell to Elisha?

5. To whom would Naaman's leprosy cleave to forever?

Important Truths:

It never pays to lie.

There are some things that money cannot buy.

What we do will affect future generations.

The Axe That Swam
II Kings 6:5-7
(Study: II Kings 6:1-7)

The sons of the prophets came to Elisha and told him the place they were staying was too small for them, and they wanted to build a new place. They asked Elisha to go with them to cut down timber for building this new dwelling place. Elisha went with them down to the Jordan River to cut down wood for building. While there, one of them was cutting down a tree and his axe head fell into the water. He told Elisha of his loss and that the axe was borrowed. Elisha asked him where it fell in the water, and he showed him. Elisha cut down a stick and threw it into the water where the axe was lost, and the iron floated to the top of the water and the man took it up.

---

1. What did the sons of the prophets want to build?

2. Whom did they ask to go with them?

3. Where did they go to cut down wood for building?

4. Why was it so important to recover the axe?

5. What did Elisha throw into the water?

> **Important Truths:**
>
> We should be willing to work for our needs.
>
> God cares about our seemingly little problems.
>
> We should be responsible for what we borrow.

Open His Eyes
II Kings 6:15-17
(Study: II Kings 6:8-17)

The king of Syria warred against the children of Israel. He made plans to lie wait in such a place to ambush Israel and their armies, but Elisha the prophet warned the king of Israel and kept him from loss many times. The king of Syria sent his army to get Elisha in the city of Dothan. When Elisha's servant saw the city surrounded, he said, "how shall we do?" Elisha told him, "Fear not: for they that be with us are more than they that be with them." Elisha then prayed for God to open his servant's eyes. When God opened his eyes, he saw the mountain full of horses, and chariots of fire round about Elisha. God protected Elisha from the Syrian army with His own army.

---

1. Who warred against Israel?

2. Who warned the king of Israel?

3. Who could not see?

4. In what city did Elisha live?

5. With what did God protect Elisha?

Important Truths:

Satan's army is no match for God's army.

Ask God to open your eyes to His plan.

God knows the secrets of man.

Close Their Eyes
II Kings 6:18-20
(Study: II Kings 6:18-23)

The king of Syria sent his army to Dothan to try to apprehend the prophet Elisha for telling the king of Israel his battle plans on several occasions, but God sent His army to protect him. Elisha asked God to smite the army of Syria with blindness, and He did so. Elisha told the blind army that he would lead them to the man that they sought. Instead, he led them all into the capital of Israel, the city of Samaria. Elisha asked the Lord to open the eyes of the enemy army, and they found themselves in the middle of Samaria. The king of Israel asked Elisha if he should kill them, but Elisha said to give them food and drink and send them back to their master, and so he did.

1. Who did the Syrian army come to arrest?

2. What did Elisha pray to happen to the Syrian army?

3. Where did Elisha lead the Syrian army?

4. Who asked if he could kill the Syrian army?

5. What did they give the Syrians before going home?

Important Truths:

Love your enemies.

God can open or close man's eyes.

Blindness makes you vulnerable.

Why Sit Here Until We Die?
II Kings 7:3-5
(Study: II Kings 6:24-7:20)

Ben-hadad the king of Syria besieged Samaria and caused a great famine in the city. There were four lepers that sat outside the gate of Samaria that were also starving to death. They decided to go to the camp of Syria to get food instead of just sitting there until they died for lack of food. When they came to the camp, it was deserted because the Lord caused those in the camp to hear the sound of horses and chariots, and they ran for fear that Israel had hired help. The four lepers went from tent to tent eating and drinking and taking gold and silver. They went and told the people in Samaria who came and spoiled the tents of the Syrians.

1. Who was the king of Syria?

2. What city was besieged and in famine?

3. How many lepers saved the city?

4. What did the lepers find at the camp of Syria?

5. Why did the Syrians run from their tents?

Important Truths:

God can use even a leper (sinner).

Soul winning is one beggar telling another beggar where the Bread is.

Believers should not just sit and do nothing.

Present Obedience, Future Reward

II Kings 8:4-6
(Study: II Kings 8:1-6)

Elisha warned the Shunammite woman that God had called for a seven-year famine, and that she and her household should go somewhere else until it was over. The Shunammite woman had been given a child as a reward for making a chamber for the prophet Elisha. That child had died and Elisha had brought him back to life. The Shunammite woman left during the famine and returned to ask the king of Israel for her house and land back. Gehazi, the servant to Elisha, was there with the king at that time, telling the story of the Shunammite woman to the king. The king sent an officer with her and restored all that was hers.

1. What prophet warned the Shunammite woman?

2. How long did the famine last?

3. What had the Shunammite woman done for Elisha?

4. Who was speaking with the king when the Shunammite woman showed up?

5. What did the king give back to the woman?

Important Truths:

God sometimes sends a famine.

God takes care of those who put Him first.

God's timing is always the right timing.

Jehu Anointed King
II Kings 9:4-6
(Study: II Kings 9:1-13)

The prophet Elisha called for one of the young prophets so he could send him to Jehu, a captain of the host of Israel. His errand was to anoint Jehu with oil to be the next king of Israel. When the young man arrived, he found Jehu sitting with the other captains of Israel and he asked to speak to Jehu privately. The young prophet anointed Jehu with oil and said, "Thus saith the LORD God of Israel, I have anointed thee king over the people of the LORD, even over Israel. And thou shalt smite the house of Ahab thy master, that I may avenge the blood of my servants the prophets, and the blood of all the servants of the LORD, at the hand of Jezebel." After the young prophet delivered his message, he quickly went away.

1. Who sent the young prophet on his errand?

2. Whom did the young prophet anoint king?

3. What was Jehu's occupation?

4. Whom was Jehu commanded to smite?

5. Whom would God avenge?

Important Truths:

God uses young men.

God raises up leaders to fulfill His will.

God rewards the evil doer for his works.

Judgement of Jezebel
II Kings 9:31-33
(Study: II Kings 9:14-37)

Jezebel, a wicked woman, was the wife of Ahab, king of Israel. She was a worshipper of Baal, and killed many of the prophets of the Lord. She devised a plan to have Naboth killed so she could steal his vineyard for her husband. Elijah, the prophet, prophesied her death for all of her evil doings. Jehu, a captain of Israel whom God said would be king, rode into Jezreel after killing Joram king of Israel, and Ahaziah, king of Judah. Jezebel looked out a window to ridicule Jehu. Jehu looked up and asked, "Who is on my side?" Three eunuchs responded, to which Jehu told them to throw her down. Jehu trampled her with his horse and left her dead body to be eaten of dogs. The Word of the Lord came to pass.

---

1. Jezebel was a worshipper of what?

2. Jezebel painted what?

3. Jezebel ridiculed whom?

4. Jezebel was thrown out of a what?

5. Jezebel was eaten by what?

Important Truths:

Sometimes it is best to keep your mouth shut.

God is a sure paymaster.

The Word of the Lord will come to pass.

Come See My Zeal
II Kings 10:15-17
(Study: II Kings 10:1-17)

Jehu, the captain of the army of Israel, was told by God that he was to be the next king. Jehu slew Jehoram the king of Israel and was come to Samaria to be king. Jehu knew that the prophet Elijah said that Ahab and his entire house would be exterminated because of his Baal worship and disregard for God. A man named Jehonadab came to meet Jehu, and Jehu said to him, "Come with me, and see my zeal for the LORD." The zeal that he was going to show him is that he would kill all that remained unto Ahab in Samaria according to the Word of the Lord by Elijah. Jehu slew all the house of Ahab by killing his great men, his kinfolk, and his priests, until he left none remaining.

---

1. Who slew Jehoram, king of Israel?

2. Who prophesied Ahab's destruction?

3. Who did Jehu invite to see his zeal for the Lord?

4. Who did Jehu kill in Samaria?

5. Jehonadab was whose son?

Important Truths:

We should be zealous to fulfill the Word of God.

We should encourage those zealous for the Lord.

We should carefully choose our associations.

Jehu Destroys Baal
II Kings 10:23-25
(Study: II Kings 10:18-36)

Jehu came to Samaria and destroyed all the house of Ahab, just like God had said by the prophet Elijah. He did not stop there. He also destroyed all the worshippers of Baal. He announced to all the people, "Ahab served Baal a little; but Jehu shall serve him much," in order to gather all the worshippers of Baal to Samaria. He organized a large gathering to supposedly do a great sacrifice to Baal, and they came and filled the house of Baal. Then Jehu gave them all a special garment to wear for the occasion. Jehu appointed eighty men to go into the house of Baal and kill all of them, and if any man let any escape, then his life was to be taken for theirs. That day Jehu destroyed Baal out of Israel.

---

1. What man prophesied Ahab's destruction?

2. Where did Jehu host his Baal gathering?

3. How many men were to kill the Baal worshippers?

4. What happened if they let one escape?

5. Jehu destroyed Baal worship out of where?

Important Truths:

You shall not have other gods before God.

Some things just need destroyed.

Leaders can make a big difference.

Hid in the House of God
II Kings 11:1-3
(Study: II Kings 11:1-12)

Ahaziah, king of Judah, was killed while God was executing judgment on Jehoram, king of Israel. After Ahaziah died, his mother Athaliah destroyed all of the children of royalty so she could reign over the land. She missed killing one of Ahaziah's children named Joash. Joash was a baby at the time of Athaliah's ruthless murder and takeover of the kingdom. For six years, Joash was hidden in the house of the Lord to protect him from Athaliah. In the seventh year, the priest Jehoiada arranged with the captains of Israel's army to protect Joash as he was made king. Jehoiada brought forth Joash, put a crown on his head, gave him the testimony, and anointed him king.

---

1. Who was Ahaziah with when he was killed?

2. Who took over Ahaziah's kingdom when he died?

3. Who killed King Ahaziah's children?

4. Who was hidden in the house of the Lord?

5. How long was he hidden there?

Important Truths:

The House of God should be a safe haven.

Covetousness can make you do the unthinkable.

Leadership needs a copy of the Word of God.

Wicked Athaliah
II Kings 11:14-16
(Study: II Kings 11:1-21)

Athaliah was the mother of King Ahaziah. When he died, Athaliah killed all the seed royal and took over the throne in Israel. Joash was the only son that God spared from her murders. The priest Jehoiada hid Joash in the house of God for six years, and in the seventh year, he called for the elders of Israel and showed them the true king of Israel. On the day that Joash was proclaimed and crowned king at the house of God, Athaliah came in crying, "Treason. Treason." Jehoiada commanded the officers of Israel to take her out of the house of God and kill her. On that day, the wicked reign of Athaliah ended, and the godly reign of seven-year-old Joash began.

---

1. Who was Athaliah's son?

2. Who hid Joash?

3. Where was Joash hidden?

4. How old was Joash when he became king?

5. What did Athaliah cry when Joash became king?

> **Important Truths:**
>
> You reap what you sow.
>
> Leadership can make a difference in the lives of tomorrow's leaders.
>
> Young people can lead with the right guidance.

Repair the House of God
II Kings 12:4-6
(Study: II Kings 12:1-16)

Joash was seven years old when he became king. He did right in the sight of the Lord all his days wherein Jehoiada the priest instructed him. When wicked Athaliah reigned over the land, she allowed the house of God to fall into disarray. Joash told the priests to take the money that people gave to repair the house of the Lord. The priests failed to do so and were reprimanded by Joash and told to take no more money. Jehoiada took a chest and put a hole in the top of it for people to give for the repairs of the house of God. After much money was collected, they gave it to faithful workmen who repaired the house of God.

---

1. Who instructed King Joash?

2. Who did Joash tell to repair the house of God?

3. How many years was Joash king at this time?

4. What did Johoiada set to collect money for the repairs?

5. Who repaired the house of God?

Important Truths:

God will use people to give above their tithes.

Spiritual leadership should take the initiative.

God's House should be kept in good repair.

Little Faith, Little Victory
II Kings 13:17-19
(Study: II Kings 13:14-25)

The prophet Elisha had become sick and was about to die. Joash, the king of Israel, came to him and said, "O my father, my father, the chariot of Israel, and horsemen thereof," which was to recognize that the man of God was the safety and protection of the nation of Israel. Israel was under attack from the Syrians. Elisha told him to shoot an arrow out the window as a symbol of Israel's deliverance. Then Elisha told Joash to hit the ground with the arrows to symbolize how much God would deliver them. Joash hit the ground three times with the arrows. Elisha reproved Joash for not doing more, and told him he would smite the Syrians in battle three times, instead of utterly destroying them.

1. What prophet had become sick unto death?

2. Who was the king of Israel?

3. Who was thought to be a protection for Israel?

4. How many times should Joash have hit the ground?

5. How many times did Israel defeat the Syrians?

Important Truths:

The man of God is an umbrella of protection.

Do what the man of God says.

Our actions demonstrate our faith.

Amaziah Wouldn't Listen
II Kings 14:11-13
(Study: II Kings 14:1-20)

Amaziah was the king of Judah and was known for doing right in the sight of the Lord. King Amaziah led his people to go to war against the Edomites and won. When he returned home, he sent messengers to Jehoash, the king of Israel, to come face him in battle. Jehoash told him that he indeed had defeated the Edomites, but if they fought, he would fall and all Judah with him. Amaziah would not listen and insisted on fighting anyway. King Jehoash came up against Amaziah and defeated him, and he went up to Judah's capital Jerusalem and broke down its wall. He took all the gold and silver in the house of God and in the king's house and returned to his home in Samaria with hostages.

---

1. Who was the king of Judah?

2. Who was the king of Israel?

3. Who did Amaziah defeat?

4. Who defeated Amaziah?

5. What wall was broken down?

Important Truths:

Pride can cause us to fall.

We should not look for a fight.

Our decisions affect more than just ourselves.

Replacement Altar
II Kings 16:10-12
(Study: II Kings 16:1-20)

Ahaz, the king of Judah, was under siege by the kings of Syria and Israel. Ahaz sent a present of gold and silver to the king of Assyria and asked for his help against them. The king of Assyria hearkened unto him and took Damascus, the capital of Syria. Ahaz went to Damascus to meet Tiglath-pileser, the king of Assyria. While there, he saw an altar that the Syrians had used for their false gods, and he sent the fashion and pattern of it to Urijah the priest in Judah, so he could replicate it. When Ahaz returned home, he went to the temple and had God's brazen altar moved and his altar put into its place. Ahaz used the brazen altar for his own use.

1. Who was the king of Judah?
2. Who was the king of Assyria?
3. Who was the priest in Judah?
4. Where was the capital of Syria?
5. What altar did the king replace in the temple?

Important Truths:

We should not replace God's things with the world's things.

Leadership sometimes does dumb things.

No one can keep God to himself.

Israel Carried into Captivity
II Kings 17:21-23
(Study: II Kings 17:1-23)

God brought the children of Israel out of Egypt by the hand of Moses. They inherited the promised land under Joshua. They asked for a king and God gave them Saul, then David, and then Solomon. Because Solomon in his old age, served idols, God rent the kingdom of Israel into two nations. Israel consisted of ten tribes of Israel and Judah was the other two. The ten tribes of Israel, could never get away from serving false gods, and would not listen to the prophets that God sent to testify against them. They were the first to go into captivity under the country of Assyria. The sins of Israel started off secretly and then ended openly. Their stiff necks and unbelief caused them to be taken into captivity.

---

1. Who were the first three kings of Israel?

2. Who caused Israel to be rent into two nations?

3. Who made Israel to "sin a great sin"?

4. What nation carried Israel away into captivity?

5. What caused Israel to be taken into captivity?

> **Important Truths:**
>
> We should listen to God's reproofs.
>
> Secret sins become open sins eventually.
>
> There are consequences to our actions.

Fearing God & Serving Images
II Kings 17:32-34
(Study: II Kings 17:24-41)

The children of Israel went into captivity under the Assyrians, and the king of Assyria sent people to repopulate their land. These people did not fear God, so the Lord sent lions among them, which killed some of them. The king of Assyria decided to send a priest back to Samaria to teach them the manner of the God of the land. The priest came and taught them how they should fear the Lord. All of these people from various nations combined their worship of false gods with fearing the Lord God Almighty. It did not last long because they soon reverted to their former manner of serving and worshipping of graven images.

---

1. Who took Israel into captivity?

2. What did God send to those who would not fear?

3. Who taught the people to fear God?

4. What did the people try to combine for worship?

5. The people reverted to their former what?

> **Important Truths:**
>
> You cannot serve God and something else.
>
> Serving God is short-lived when combined with worldly practices.
>
> You cannot teach spirituality to a lost person.

Revival under Hezekiah
II Kings 18:5-7
(Study: II Kings 18:1-12)

Hezekiah was the son of Ahaz, king of Judah. Ahaz did not do that which was right in the sight of the Lord, but Hezekiah did. When he became king, he broke in pieces the graven images and clave to the Lord. Because of Hezekiah's obedience, God made him to prosper whithersoever he went. He had victory over the Philistines and stopped serving the Assyrians. Because of Hezekiah's trust in God and obedience to Him, there was not another king of Judah like him, before or after him. While God was blessing Hezekiah for his obedience, he punished the rest of Israel for their disobedience and sent them into captivity under the Assyrians.

---

1. Who was Hezekiah's father?

2. Was he a good king?

3. What did Hezekiah break in pieces?

4. What made Hezekiah like no other king of Judah?

5. Whom did the Assyrians take into captivity?

> **Important Truths:**
>
> You don't have to copy bad parenting.
>
> God blesses faith and obedience.
>
> God punishes unbelief and disobedience.

Sennacherib Attacks Jerusalem
II Kings 18:29-31
(Study: II Kings 18:13-37)

Sennacherib was the king of Assyria and came up against Hezekiah, king of Judah. Sennacherib sent his captains to Jerusalem to ask Hezekiah to surrender. His captains met outside Jerusalem's wall with Hezekiah's representatives, to give a message to their master. When they recognized they had an audience with the soldiers on the wall, they tried to put fear in them. They began to ridicule their leader Hezekiah, and told them that they should not listen to Hezekiah, or let him deceive them, or make them trust in the Lord for deliverance. Instead, he said that they should surrender and that Assyria would give them a land like their own land.

---

1. Who was the king of Assyria?

2. Who was the king of Judah?

3. In whom did Hezekiah want the people to trust?

4. In whom did the Assyrian captain try to put fear?

5. What did Assyria offer if Judah would surrender?

Important Truths:

Our adversary will try to put us in fear.

Our adversary will try to downgrade authority.

Our adversary will try to offer something better.

God Delivers Jerusalem
II Kings 19:33-35
(Study: II Kings 19:1-37)

Sennacherib, king of Assyria, came up against Hezekiah at Jerusalem and tried to get him to surrender the city to him. Hezekiah went to Isaiah the prophet to get counsel from God. God told Hezekiah that he did not need to fear and that God would cause the king of Assyria to fall. Sennacherib had become proud because of all of his military victories, and did not realize that it was God Who gave them to him. God sent His angel into the camp of the Assyrians and killed 185,000 of their host. Sennacherib went back home in shame and there two of his sons killed him while he was worshipping in the house of his false gods.

1. To what prophet did Hezekiah go for answers?

2. Whom did God send to destroy the Assyrians?

3. How many Assyrians did God spare?

4. Who killed Sennacherib?

5. For whose sake did God save Jerusalem?

Important Truths:

All of the victories in life are because of God.

When you need an answer, go to God.

If you fight against God, you will lose.

Set Thine House in Order
II Kings 20:1-3
(Study: II Kings 20:1-11)

Hezekiah was a good king of the nation of Judah. When he became king, he removed the idols, trusted and clave to the Lord, and the Lord was with him. The Lord allowed Hezekiah to become sick and sent Isaiah to tell him that he was going to die and that he should set his house in order. Hezekiah wept and prayed for God to heal him, and God did. Isaiah the prophet returned and told him that God said he would lengthen his days, and he would live another fifteen years. Hezekiah asked Isaiah what would be the sign that God would heal him. Isaiah asked God to bring the sun backward ten degrees, to assure Hezekiah that God would heal him. So God moved the sun backward!

---

1. From what prophet did Hezekiah get direction?

2. What did Hezekiah do that made him a good king?

3. What did Hezekiah ask God to remember?

4. How many more years did God give Hezekiah?

5. What did God do to assure Hezekiah of his healing?

Important Truths:

Man's life and health are in God's hand.

It is important to set your house in order before you die.

God knows exactly how long we will live.

The Kids Can Pay for It
II Kings 20:17-19
(Study: II Kings 20:12-21)

Hezekiah was a good king of Judah. Toward the end of his life, he made a sad mistake. The king of Babylon sent letters and a present to him because he heard that Hezekiah was sick. When his representatives came, Hezekiah showed them all his silver, gold, precious things, armor, and all the things that were in his treasuries. God sent the prophet Isaiah to Hezekiah to tell him that what he did was wrong. He said that the day would come that the king of Babylon would take all that was in his house and his children would be taken captive. Hezekiah's response was, "Good is the word of the LORD...Is it not good, if peace and truth be in my days?" In other words, it is good because I will not have to pay for it.

---

1. Who sent a letter and present to Hezekiah?

2. What did Hezekiah show to the Babylonians?

3. Who did God send to reprove Hezekiah?

4. Who would be taken captive for Hezekiah's folly?

5. What two things did Hezekiah want in his days of life?

Important Truths:

Decisions today will affect others tomorrow.

All that we have belongs to God.

Pride can make us do some dumb things.

Not Like His Father
II Kings 21:1-3
(Study: II Kings 21:1-18)

Hezekiah was a good king of Judah that "did that which was right in the sight of the LORD" (II Kings 18:3). However, he had a son named Manasseh that "did that which was evil in the sight of the LORD." Manasseh was so evil that he even made his son go into the fire as a sacrifice to false gods. God said of Manasseh that he "shed innocent blood very much, till he had filled Jerusalem from one end to another." God warned Manasseh of his wrong doing and its consequences, but he would not listen. Manasseh had one of the best examples of a king and father, but chose not to follow or do what he had been taught. The Lord forsook Israel for their sin.

---

1. How old was Manasseh when he began to reign?

2. Who was Manasseh's father?

3. What did Manasseh sacrifice to false gods?

4. With what did Manasseh fill Jerusalem?

5. What would God do because of Israel's sin?

> **Important Truths:**
>
> Good parents do not guarantee good children.
>
> Bad leadership will affect a nation.
>
> You can make the decision you want, but you have no control over the consequences.

Just Like His Father
II Kings 21:19-21
(Study: II Kings 21:19-26)

It has been said "the fruit does not fall far from the tree," and "he is a chip off of the old block." Those statements are usually to indicate that a son turned out just like his father. There is a natural tendency to follow in our father's footsteps whether they are good or bad. Amon took over as king of Judah after his father Manasseh. Of both it was said that they "did that which was evil in the sight of the LORD." Amon served his father's idols and forsook the Lord. Amon's choice to do evil did not last long because he was killed by his own servants in his own house after serving as king for only two years in Jerusalem.

1. Who was Amon's father?

2. Where was Amon king?

3. What was said about both Amon and his father?

4. How long was Amon king?

5. Who killed Amon?

Important Truths:

Sons tend to follow in their father's footsteps.

Everyone can choose which path they will take.

A father's relationship with God can determine his son's relationship with God.

Josiah Finds the Book
II Kings 22:11-13
(Study: II Kings 22:1-20)

Josiah was eight years old when he became king in Jerusalem and did that which was right in the sight of the Lord. His father and grandfather were kings that did evil in the sight of the Lord and served idols. When Josiah was twenty-six years old he called for men to repair the house of the Lord. In so doing, they found the book of the law and read it before Josiah. When he heard what God was going to do to Israel for forsaking Him and serving idols, he rent his clothes, humbled himself, prayed and sent to inquire of the Lord. God told him that because his heart was tender that he would die in peace and that God's judgement against Israel would come after his reign.

1. How old was Josiah when he became king?

2. How old was Josiah when he repaired God's house?

3. What was found in the house of God?

4. Why was God's judgment against Israel?

5. What did Josiah do when he heard God's Word?

Important Truths:

Young people can have tender hearts towards God.

The House of God is a place to find God's Word.

God's Word should humble us.

Josiah's Promise
II Kings 23:1-3
(Study: II Kings 23:1-20)

Josiah was one of the greatest kings of Israel. In the eighteenth year of his reign, he found the book of the law in the house of God, and it changed his life. Because his heart was tender and obedient, God showed mercy on him and let him have a peaceful reign. Josiah called all the people together and read the book of the law and made a covenant promise to God after reading it. His promise was threefold: to walk after the Lord, to keep his commandments, and to perform the words of the book. When Josiah declared his promise to God, all the people stood to the covenant, and immediately destroyed idols, graven images, false altars, and the houses of the sodomites.

---

1. What changed Josiah's life?

2. What did Josiah read to the people?

3. What was Josiah's threefold promise?

4. What did the people do when Josiah covenanted?

5. What did Josiah do after making his promise to God?

Important Truths:

God's Word will provoke a decision.

Action is the fulfillment of promises.

Our personal decisions will affect the decisions of others.

Josiah Was One of a Kind
II Kings 23:23-25
(Study: II Kings 23:21-30)

Josiah was a great king of Judah. Israel's ten tribes had already gone into captivity under Assyria, which left the land of Judah with the other two tribes of Israel. The Israelites had followed the path of idol worship just like their brethren in the region of Samaria. When Josiah became king at age eight, he inherited from his father a kingdom that had forsaken God. When Josiah read in the book of law what God had said, he turned to Him with all of his heart and led Israel to do the same. God said of Josiah that there was no king before or after him that turned to the Lord with all his heart, like he had. Josiah would be forever remembered as a good king of Israel because of his fervor for God.

1. Who took the first ten tribes into captivity?

2. How old was Josiah when he became king?

3. For what would Josiah be known?

4. For what was Josiah's father known?

5. What caused Josiah to turn to God with all his heart?

Important Truths:

We will be remembered for how we love God.

Our personal legacy will be our actions for God.

We can change our family's former reputation.

Judah Carried into Captivity
II Kings 25:7-9
(Study: II Kings 25:1-21)

Zedekiah king of Judah would not listen to the prophet Jeremiah and turn from his wickedness. So God sent Nebuchadnezzar king of Babylon against him. Nebuchadnezzar besieged Jerusalem for a year and a half until the city was broken up because of famine. Zedekiah tried to escape but was caught and brought to judgment. Nebuchadnezzar killed Zedekiah's sons before him, then put out his eyes, and bound him in chains to be taken back to Babylon. Before leaving, Nebuchadnezzar burned the house of the Lord, the kings house, and then broke down the walls of Jerusalem. The Israelites in Judah were taken captive to Babylon and would be there for the next seventy years.

---

1. Who was the king of Babylon?

2. What prophet would Zedekiah not heed?

3. What happened to Zedekiah for his disobedience?

4. How long would Judah be in captivity?

5. What was burned down in Jerusalem?

Important Truths:

Reproof is God's warning to get right.

It is wise to listen to God's man.

You cannot escape God's judgment.

The Prayer of Jabez
I Chronicles 4:9-11
(Study: I Chronicles 4:9-20)

There are only two verses in the whole Bible that actually talk about this man named Jabez. His mother bare him in sorrow, thus his name means to grieve or be sorrowful. In this man's two verse biography, we see a prayer and God's answer to that prayer. Jabez asked God for four things: for God to bless him; to enlarge his coasts; to put His hand with him; and to keep him from evil. Jabez received all four things, because the Bible says, "And God granted him that which he requested." We know nothing else about Jabez except his personal prayer and how God recognized it in the genealogies of Israel. Jabez' life might have began sadly, but it ended happily because he prayed.

---

1. Jabez was more honorable than whom?

2. What does Jabez mean?

3. For what four things did Jabez pray?

4. What did God grant to Jabez?

5. How many verses in the Bible are about Jabez?

Important Truths:

God may grant our desires, if we only request.

We should pray for God to bless us.

Prayer makes us honorable to others.

Why Saul Died

I Chronicles 10:12-14
(Study: I Chronicles 10:1-14)

Before Saul became king of Israel, God said, "there was not among the children of Israel a goodlier person than he" (I Samuel 9:2). After Saul became king, Saul changed. Pride turned him into another man. The prophet Samuel warned Saul, "When thou wast little in thine own sight, wast thou not made the head of the tribes of Israel." Saul did several things wrong when he was king, but God specifically noted two things that caused him to lose the kingship. The first one was when he directly disobeyed God and did not utterly destroy the Amalekites. The other was when he went to the witch of Endor to get counsel. Saul and his sons died in battle and God gave the throne to David.

---

1. Whom did God call a goodly person?

2. What changed Saul into another man?

3. What prophet warned Saul of wrong doing?

4. What two things did God say that Saul did wrong?

5. To whom did God give the kingdom after Saul?

Important Truths:

Pride will ruin any man.

Everyone is capable of going from good to bad.

Our sin can cost our families too.

David's Helpers
I Chronicles 12:21-23
(Study: I Chronicles 11:1-12:40)

After Saul died in battle the Bible says, "So David waxed greater and greater; for the LORD of hosts was with him" (I Chronicles 11:9). Every day, the Lord would send someone to help David until he had a great host of men. These men were strong and courageous. God used these men to deliver David and Israel at times of war. God described them as men that were "expert in war…could keep rank…not of a double heart…and men that had understanding of the times." One of David's mighty men was Jashobeam who killed three hundred men at one time. Another was Benaiah who slew a lion. David was a great king because of the great help God gave him!

1. Who was with David that made him great?

2. How are David's helpers described?

3. Who killed three hundred men at one time?

4. Who killed a lion?

5. Whose host was David's great host like?

Important Truths:

Great men are often surrounded by great help.

God sees the qualities of those who are helpers.

Good help is sent from God.

Do It Right
I Chronicles 13:9-11
(Study: I Chronicles 13:1-15:29)

King David gathered Israel together to bring up the ark of the covenant from Kirjath-jearim to Jerusalem. In so doing, he had Uzza and Ahio put the ark on a cart to transport it. Uzza put his hand on the ark to steady it and God killed him. David was afraid of God that day and placed the ark in the house of Obed-edom instead of bringing it back to Jerusalem. After three months, David decided to bring the ark the rest of the way to Jerusalem, but this time he would do it the right way. He knew he had done wrong by transporting it by a cart and not having the Levites carry it. The Levites brought the ark to Jerusalem with joy and singing.

---

1. From where was the ark being transported?

2. To where was the ark being taken?

3. Who touched the ark of the covenant?

4. What happened to the man who touched the ark?

5. Who was supposed to carry the ark?

> **Important Truths:**
>
> Doing right things the right way, is important.
>
> God takes seriously how we keep His commands.
>
> We should learn from our mistakes.

Satan Provokes David
I Chronicles 21:1-3
(Study: I Chronicles 21:1-30)

Satan provoked David to number the children of Israel because he was against Israel. Satan was not attacking David, but the Israelites. David did not realize what the Devil was doing when he numbered Israel. David's act of pride was discouraged by his captain Joab, but David would not listen. After receiving Israel's census, God sent the prophet Gad to David to choose his punishment from either famine, foes, or pestilence. David chose to fall into the hand of God and go through three days of pestilence. God killed 70,000 Israelites and David said to God, it is I that have sinned and done this evil. God ceased the destruction and David built an altar to the Lord.

---

1. Satan stood up against whom?

2. Who did David tell to number the people?

3. What prophet did God send to David?

4. What three options of punishment did David have?

5. How many Israelites were killed for David's sin?

> **Important Truths:**
>
> Satan can use us to get to others.
>
> God is more pleased by obedience than numbers.
>
> Even leadership is tempted to sin and we should pray for them.

David Prepares before Death
I Chronicles 22:5-7
(Study: I Chronicles 22:1-19)

King David is getting old and he had a desire to build a house for the Lord. God told David he could not build the house because he had shed much blood in war. However, God said that David would have a son named Solomon that would build the house of God. Before David died, he made much preparation for the house of God that his son Solomon would build. He gathered iron, brass, gold, and silver in abundance to have the material ready for constructing the Lord's house. David charged Solomon to build the house of God and told him of his preparations for it. David also commanded all the princes of Israel to help his son Solomon build the sanctuary of the Lord.

1. David charged Solomon to do what to God's house?

2. What was in David's mind to do?

3. What did David gather abundantly for building?

4. Who did God say would build the house of God?

5. Who did David command to help Solomon build?

Important Truths:

We should help the next generation build for God.

Just because we have a desire to do something, does not mean it is God's will.

We cannot always build, but we can help others to build.

David's Counsel to Solomon
I Chronicles 28:19-21
(Study: I Chronicles 28:1-21)

King David gives his last known counsel to Solomon. He tells him the pattern of the temple and the will of God for it to be built. David encourages Solomon by telling him, "Be strong and of good courage, and do it: fear not, nor be dismayed: for the LORD God, even my God, will be with thee." David also told Solomon that God told him, "I will establish his kingdom for ever, if he be constant to do my commandments and my judgments, as at this day" (v. 7). David wanted Solomon to succeed as king and knew his success would come by obedience to the Word of the Lord. David told Solomon he would not be alone in his endeavor but that the priests, Levites, princes, and the people would help him.

1. David gave Solomon the pattern for what?

2. What would establish Solomon's kingdom?

3. Who would help Solomon build the temple?

4. Who gave David the understanding for the temple?

5. How would Solomon succeed?

Important Truths:

The young men should obey the counsel of the old men.

We should accept the help God gives us.

Obedience and consistency are necessary for success.

Offering of Thanksgiving
I Chronicles 29:14-16
(Study: I Chronicles 29:1-22)

David is at the end of life and his reign as king. David gives an offering that he had prepared for the house of the Lord. He then asks the Israelites, "Who then is willing to consecrate his service this day unto the Lord?" The priests and the people both gave willingly an offering to the Lord for the house of God. David praised the Lord that God had given them so much, that they could give back to Him what He had given them for an offering to build the temple. Six times in the story the Bible says that they offered willingly to the Lord. They all took part in giving and then praised the Lord that they were able to do so.

1. Who initiated and gave to the offering first?

2. Who did David ask if they were willing to give?

3. How many times does it say they offered willingly?

4. Who gave the people the ability to give?

5. What was their offering for?

Important Truths:

Leadership should give first.

God loves a cheerful giver.

All that we have comes from God.

This Was in Thine Heart
II Chronicles 1:10-12
(Study: II Chronicles 1:1-17)

Solomon had just become king and he and the people had gone up to Gibeon and offered unto the Lord a thousand sacrifices. That night the Lord appeared unto Solomon and said, "Ask what I shall give thee." Solomon's answer was for God to give him wisdom to lead and judge God's people Israel. God responded, "Because this was in thine heart," He would give him wisdom, but also riches, wealth, and honor. Solomon did not have in his heart to be rich or an all-powerful ruler, but that he would have the God given ability to lead the children of Israel in the right path. God knew what was in the heart of Solomon, and because it was good, God granted his desire.

---

1. Where was Solomon when God appeared to him?

2. How many sacrifices did Solomon offer to God?

3. For what two things did Solomon ask God?

4. Who did Solomon consider to be great?

5. What did God give Solomon besides wisdom?

Important Truths:

God sees what is in our hearts.

Wisdom should be the principle thing in our lives.

God can give more than our heart's desire.

Send Me a Man
II Chronicles 2:7-9
(Study: II Chronicles 2:1-18)

Solomon became king after David, his father, and determined to build the house of the Lord, like his father had charged him. Solomon sent to Huram, the king of Tyre, for help in building the house of the Lord. The two things that he asked for was a skillful man and timber. Huram was pleased to help Solomon and sent him a man that was skillful in gold, silver, brass, iron, stone, timber, and linen. This man would also be able "to find out every device which shall be put to him." Huram also promised to send him as much wood as he would need. Solomon in return gave to Huram for his work and timber; wheat, barley, wine, and oil.

---

1. From which king did Solomon ask for help?

2. What two things did Solomon ask for?

3. What did Solomon need help to do?

4. The man Huram sent had what skills?

5. With what did Solomon pay Huram for his help?

> **Important Truths:**
>
> Wise men need skillful help.
>
> We should be willing to pay for what we need.
>
> Men who can figure things out are rare.

One Altar
II Chronicles 4:6-8
(Study: II Chronicles 4:1-22)

Not long after Solomon became king, he began to construct the house of God using David's pattern. This temple would truly be magnificent. The tabernacle was a portable place of worship for Israel. The temple would be a permanent place of worship. There were more than a few changes from the tabernacle to the new temple. Instead of one laver, one golden candlestick, and one table of showbread, there would be ten of each in the new house of God. One thing Solomon did not duplicate multiple times was the brazen altar (v. 1). The brazen altar is the place Israel would bring their blood sacrifices and was a picture of the cross of Christ.

1. Who gave Solomon the pattern for the temple?

2. What was a portable place of worship for Israel?

3. What was the permanent place of worship?

4. What did Solomon have ten of in the temple?

5. Of what was the brazen altar a picture?

Important Truths:

Jesus is the only sacrifice for sin.

God's house should be first class.

Things can be beautiful and still be right.

God Fills the House
II Chronicles 5:11-13
(Study: II Chronicles 5:1-14)

Solomon finished building the house of the Lord and assembled the children of Israel together to dedicate it. The Levites brought into it all the holy vessels and the ark of the covenant. Inside the ark of the covenant were the two tables of stone containing the 10 commandments. The congregation sacrificed sheep and oxen to God that could not be numbered because there were so many. Then they began to praise and thank God saying, "For he is good; for his mercy endureth for ever." Then the glory of the Lord in the form of a cloud, filled the house of God, so that even the priests could not stand to minister in the temple.

1. What was it that Solomon dedicated to God?

2. Who brought in the ark of the covenant?

3. What was inside the ark of the covenant?

4. What did the people say when they praised God?

5. The glory of God was in the form of what?

Important Truths:

God's house is a special place.

God's house should be filled with His praises.

God's house is where we bring our sacrifices.

Prayer of Solomon
II Chronicles 6:18-20
(Study: II Chronicles 6:1-42)

After Solomon built the temple and brought the people together to dedicate it, he made a public prayer to the Lord. Solomon kneeled and raised his hands toward Heaven to dedicate the temple to God. He realized that the building of the temple was God's doing and that he was just a tool to have it built. Solomon, in his prayer to God, went through several scenarios of when the Israelites would pray to God, or in the new temple and asked for God to hear and to answer their requests. Solomon knew there would be times that Israel would sin, but also knew God could forgive them if they would pray. Solomon wanted the temple to be a place Israel could go, to get God's ear.

---

1. Was Solomon's prayer public or private?

2. How was Solomon positioned when he prayed?

3. What cannot contain God?

4. Who was just a tool in the building of the temple?

5. Solomon knew Israel would sin and need what?

Important Truths:

God's house is a house of prayer.

The church is a dedicated place to meet with God.

Anything God is associated with, is sacred.

Promise for Revival

II Chronicles 7:12-14
(Study: II Chronicles 7:1-22)

Solomon dedicated the new temple with sacrifice and prayer. God heard Solomon's prayer and appeared unto him at night and made him a promise! If Israel were to sin and be punished, that God would hear their prayer, forgive their sin, and heal their land. There was a prerequisite though, for this to happen. God's people had to humble themselves, pray, seek His face, and turn from their wicked ways. Just as Israel was chosen by God to be His people, so is every believer that has become His child (John 15:16). We, like Israel, can go through periods of backsliding. God promises a revival if we return to Him in a right manner.

---

1. When did God come to Solomon?

2. What four things must we do to see revival?

3. What three things will God do if we return to Him?

4. God chose the temple to be a house of what?

5. Besides Israel, who else has God chosen to be His people?

Important Truths:

Sin will bring God's displeasure and punishment.

God is forgiving if we will return to Him.

Revival is possible.

Separate and Strengthen
II Chronicles 11:15-17
(Study: II Chronicles 11:1-17)

After Solomon died, the kingdom of Israel split in two; the northern kingdom, which was led by Jeroboam, and the southern kingdom by Rehoboam, the son of Solomon. Jeroboam did evil in the sight of the Lord and set up golden calves to be Israel's gods. Rehoboam did right by following in the way of King David and Solomon. All those in Israel who set their hearts to seek the Lord left Jeroboam in the Northern kingdom and came to Rehoboam in the Southern kingdom. By doing this, they made Rehoboam strong. The strength of Rehoboam's kingdom was the people who had set their hearts to seek the Lord.

---

1. Who was the leader of the northern kingdom?

2. Who was the leader of the southern kingdom?

3. What did Jeroboam set up to be Israel's gods?

4. How long did Rehoboam walk in the way of his father Solomon?

5. What was the strength of Rehoboam's kingdom?

Important Truths:

Separation is a personal and necessary choice.

There is strength in spiritual people.

Godly people look for godly leadership.

An Unprepared Heart
II Chronicles 12:12-14
(Study: II Chronicles 12:1-16)

King Rehoboam was strengthened because he sought the Lord. Yet, after three years, he forsook the law of God and all Israel with him. In the fifth year of Rehoboam's reign, the Lord sent Shishak, king of Egypt up against him, with a great number of people, who took the fenced cities of Judah and came up against Jerusalem. God sent the prophet Shemaiah to Rehoboam to show him his loss was because he had forsaken the Lord. Rehoboam humbled himself and the Lord gave him deliverance, but Shishak took all the treasures of the king's house and the house of the Lord. The invasion by the Egyptians was a result of Rehoboam's not preparing his heart to seek the Lord.

1. How many years did Rehoboam do right?

2. Who was the king of Egypt?

3. Who was the prophet that warned Rehoboam?

4. Why did God give Rehoboam deliverance?

5. What did the king of Egypt take from Jerusalem?

Important Truths:

Strength is not in numbers, but in God.

God can promote a man or put him down.

Pride can cause a lot of trouble and heartache.

Ought Ye Not to Know
II Chronicles 13:3-5
(Study: II Chronicles 13:1-19)

Abijah was the king of Judah and God was their Captain. Jeroboam was the king of Israel that served golden calves. The two of them came to battle against each other. Abijah had 400,000 men and Jeroboam had 800,000 men. Before the battle began, Abijah spoke to Jeroboam and said, "Ought ye not to know" that God is with us because we have not forsaken Him, and that they had cast out the priests and served golden calves. Jeroboam did not care and set up an ambushment against Judah and had his men before and behind Judah. The men of Judah cried unto the Lord and He smote Jeroboam and all Israel before Judah. Then 500,000 of Jeroboam's army fell down slain.

---

1. Who was Abijah?

2. Who was Jeroboam?

3. How many men were with Judah?

4. How many men were with Israel?

5. How many men of Israel died in the battle?

Important Truths:

Whoever is with God has the majority.

Some people refuse to do what they know is right.

Man's plans cannot change God's purpose.

Asa Goes to Battle
II Chronicles 14:10-12
(Study: II Chronicles 14:1-15)

After Abijah, the king of Judah died, his son Asa reigned in his stead. Asa did that which was good and right in the sight of the Lord. For the first ten years, he had peace because the Lord had given him rest. Shortly thereafter came Zerah, an Ethiopian with a million-man army. The Ethiopians outnumbered Asa's army by almost two to one. Asa cried unto the Lord and asked for His help and told the Lord that they were resting on Him for deliverance. God came through for Asa and smote the Ethiopians before Asa, and before Judah. Asa pursued those who fled, and carried away much spoil.

---

1. Who was Asa's father?

2. Asa became the king of what country?

3. Who came up to fight against Asa?

4. How many men did they bring to the battle?

5. Who did Asa rest upon for deliverance?

Important Truths:

The Lord can save by many or by few.

Both peaceful years and victory in battle come from God.

It is better to be right with God before a battle.

Don't Be Without
II Chronicles 15:2-4
(Study: II Chronicles 15:1-19)

After King Asa returned from victory over the Ethiopians, he was met by the prophet Azariah. Azariah told them that as long as they sought the Lord, He would be found of them, but if they forsook God, He would forsake them. He also told them that for a long time Israel had been without the true God, a teaching priest, and the law. It was during those times that they were without those things, that they had no peace, great vexation, and all adversity. When Asa heard the words of Azariah, he took courage and put away all the abominable idols in the land, and made a covenant with all Judah to seek the Lord God with all their hearts. The Lord was found of them, and He gave them rest.

1. What prophet gave a warning to Asa?

2. What was the prophet's warning?

3. What three things had Israel been without?

4. What did Asa put away out of the land?

5. What did Asa make a covenant to do?

Important Truths:

Don't be without God.

Don't be without a man of God.

Don't be without the Word of God.

Rely on the Lord
II Chronicles 16:7-9
(Study: II Chronicles 16:1-14)

Baasha, king of Israel came up against Asa, king of Judah and would not allow anyone to come in or out of Jerusalem. Asa sent money to Ben-hadad, king of Syria to get his help, and he did. Baasha retreated to his own land, but God was not pleased with Asa for getting help from a heathen king. God sent the prophet Hanani to Asa to reprove him for not relying on the Lord for help, and to remind him of how God delivered him twenty years ago from the huge host of the Ethiopians. Asa became angry with the prophet and put him in prison. God smote Asa with a disease in his feet, but he still would not look to the Lord, but to physicians. The disease took his life.

1. Who was the king of Israel?

2. Who was the king of Judah?

3. Who was the king of Syria?

4. Who was the prophet that reproved Asa?

5. What happened to Asa for not accepting reproof?

Important Truths:

Sometimes we forget what God has done for us.

We should rely upon God and not man.

What we do with reproof can make or break us.

Joining the World
II Chronicles 18:1-3
(Study: II Chronicles 17:1-18:3)

Jehoshaphat was the son of Asa, king of Judah. When he became king he "strengthened himself against Israel." He immediately sought the Lord and began to teach in the cities of Judah the Book of the Law. The Lord blessed Jehoshaphat with riches and honor, and established the kingdom in His hand. After some time, he made a bad mistake by going down to Samaria where Ahab the king of Israel lived. Not only did he visit him, but made an alliance with the man against whom a few years earlier he had set up a defense. Jehoshaphat allowed his growing power to dim his sight concerning Israel's wickedness.

---

1. Jehoshaphat was the son of whom?

2. What was the first thing Jehoshaphat did as king?

3. What did Jehoshaphat have taught throughout the cities of Judah?

4. With what did the Lord bless Jehoshaphat?

5. Who did Jehoshaphat join affinity with?

Important Truths:

We should set up a defense against worldly things.

God blesses those who lift up His Book, the Bible.

Time and prosperity can blind us to the enemy.

A True Man of God
II Chronicles 18:11-13
(Study: II Chronicles 18:1-34)

Ahab, the king of Israel, asked Jehoshaph, the king of Judah, to join him in battle against the Syrians. Jehoshaphat asked Ahab to enquire of the Lord if they should do so. Ahab brought his 400 prophets before Jehoshaphat who said they would win in battle. Jehoshaphat asked Ahab if there was a prophet of the Lord besides these. Ahab told him there was one named Micaiah, but that he hated him because he never prophesied good concerning himself. Micaiah was brought before both kings and he told them that if they went to battle against the Syrians, that they would surely fall. Ahab did not like his prophesy and put him in jail and went to war anyway. Ahab died in battle because he would not listen.

---

1. Who was the king of Israel?

2. Who was the king of Judah?

3. How many false prophets were with Ahab?

4. Who was the true man of God?

5. Who hated the man of God?

Important Truths:

There are many false prophets.

There are few true men of God.

Real men of God are often hated for their stand.

Jehoshaphat Reproved

II Chronicles 19:1-3
(Study: II Chronicles 19:1-11)

Jehoshaphat, the king of Judah, went down to Ahab, the king of Israel, and helped him in a battle against the Syrians. They lost the battle and Jehoshaphat barely escaped with his life. When he returned to Jerusalem, he was met by Jehu the son of the prophet Hanani. Jehu reproved Jehoshaphat for helping Ahab who was ungodly and hated the Lord. Jehoshaphat accepted the reproof and brought the people back to the Lord. He set up judges throughout the land and told them to judge in the fear of the Lord. He reminded them that they were not judging for man, but for the Lord. He told the judges not to do three things: no iniquity; no respect of persons; and no taking of gifts.

---

1. Who reproved Jehoshaphat?

2. What did Jehoshaphat do wrong?

3. What did Jehoshaphat set up to help the people?

4. For whom is a judge really judging?

5. What three things should a judge not do?

Important Truths:

Good people sometimes do dumb things.

Accepting reproof makes one wise.

Judges have a great responsibility.

Not Knowing What to Do
II Chronicles 20:10-12
(Study: II Chronicles 20:1-37)

Jehoshaphat was a good king of Judah. One day, three nations came up against him to battle. They were the children of Ammon, Moab, and Mount Seir. This great multitude caused Jehoshaphat to fear and he did not know what to do. So Jehoshaphat did the only thing he knew to do, and that was to seek the Lord. The Lord answered him through a Levite named Jahaziel who said, "Be not afraid nor dismayed by reason of this great multitude; for the battle is not your's, but God's." The next day they went out to battle and when they began to sing, the Lord worked on their behalf. God caused the children of Ammon and Moab to destroy the inhabitants of Mount Sier, and then each other.

---

1. What three nations came up against Jehoshaphat?

2. What did Jehoshaphat do first in his crisis?

3. Through whom did God answer Jehoshaphat?

4. God destroyed the enemy when Judah did what?

5. How did the three enemy nations die in battle?

Important Truths:

There are times that you do not know what to do.

God always is available and capable of anything.

Sing when you are in a crisis.

Departed Undesired
II Chronicles 21:18-20
(Study: II Chronicles 21:1-20)

The good king of Judah, Jehoshaphat, passed away and his son Jehoram reigned in his stead. Jehoram married the daughter of Ahab and as soon as he became king, he slew all of his brothers. Jehoram forsook God and did much evil in the sight of the Lord. He compelled Judah to commit immorality and serve false gods. The prophet Elijah sent him a letter and told him that because he made Judah to go astray and killed his brethren, that God would smite him with a great plague. Moreover, the Lord sent the Philistines and the Arabians to break into the king's house and take away all his substance, his sons, and his wives. After two years, Jehoram died of an incurable disease without being desired.

1. Who was Jehoram's father?

2. Who did Jehoram marry?

3. Who did Jehoram murder?

4. Who wrote to Jehoram and reproved him of his sin?

5. Who stole Jehoram's substance, sons, and wives?

Important Truths:

Sometimes God's punishment is not immediate, but it is sure.

We can heed or reject God's letter to us.

Be careful whom you marry.

Counseled to Destruction
II Chronicles 22:2-4
(Study: II Chronicles 22:1-12)

After Jehoram, king of Judah, passed away, his son Ahaziah took over. Like his father, he was not a good king. Ahaziah's mother was Athaliah, who was the sister of Ahab. She counselled him to do wickedly and caused him to do evil in the sight of the Lord. His ungodliness brought swift destruction. Ahaziah was killed by Jehu when he went down to Samaria to see Jehoram the son of Ahab. When Athaliah saw her son was dead, she went and destroyed all the royal seed of the house of Judah, so she could reign over the land. She missed one child of the seed royal named Joash, but for six years she reigned over the land.

1. Who was Ahaziah's father?

2. Ahaziah became king of what country?

3. Who was Ahaziah's mother?

4. Who counselled Ahaziah to do wickedly?

5. Who killed Ahaziah?

Important Truths:

We should seek counsel carefully.

There are good and bad counselors.

Ungodly family can lead you astray.

Jehoiada the Priest
II Chronicles 23:13-15
(Study: II Chronicles 23:1-21)

Athaliah reigned for six years and then the priest Jehoiada put a stop to it. Jehoiada had been protecting and raising Joash, the king's son, in the house of God. Athaliah had murdered all of the seed royal except for Joash who was hidden by Jehoiada. Jehoiada gathered the captains of Judah's army and made a covenant with them to have the king's son reign as the Lord said. Jehoiada and the captains brought out the king's son, Joash, and put a crown on his head, and the testimony in his hand, and made him king. Athaliah did not like it and cried treason, but Jehoiada had her executed. Then Jehoiada made a covenant between all the people and Joash that they would be the Lord's people!

1. Who reigned over Judah for six years?

2. Who did Jehoiada hide in the house of God?

3. Why did Queen Athaliah cry "treason"?

4. What two things was the new king given?

5. What covenant did Joash and all the people make?

Important Truths:

Leadership, good or bad, will change a nation.

Raising one good child can help change a nation.

Good leadership will have the testimony of God.

Forgetting Kindnesses
II Chronicles 24:20-22
(Study: II Chronicles 24:1-27)

Joash was seven years old when he began to reign and he reigned forty years in Jerusalem. Joash did right in sight of the Lord all the days of Jehoiada the priest. After Jehoiada passed away, the princes of Judah came to him and caused him to serve idols. The Lord sent prophets to Joash to bring him back, but he refused to listen. Finally, Zechariah the son of Jehoiada rebuked the inhabitants of Jerusalem and said, "Because ye have forsaken the LORD, he hath also forsaken you." Joash commanded for Zechariah to be stoned to death, and did not remember the kindness that his father had done for him by saving his life and making him king.

---

1. How long did Joash reign?

2. Joash did right as long as who was alive?

3. Who caused Joash to turn from God?

4. Who rebuked Joash for his turning from God?

5. What kindness did Joash forget?

Important Truths:

Time can cause us to forget our spiritual heritage.

Worldly influences can cause us to forget our spiritual mentors.

Idolatry will cause us to forget God.

What About the Money
II Chronicles 25:7-9
(Study: II Chronicles 25:1-28)

Amaziah was the king of Judah and decided to go to battle against the Edomites. Since he did not want to go alone, he hired the other ten tribes of Israel to go with him to battle. A man of God came to Amaziah and warned him that God was not with Israel and if they went with him to the battle, he would fall. Amaziah had already paid the army of Israel an hundred talents to go with him. The man of God reminded Amaziah that God could give him much more than this, so Amaziah sent the army of Israel home. Then Amaziah went to war against the Edomites and destroyed them in battle. Unfortunately, Amaziah made an even greater mistake because he brought back to Judah the gods of Edom.

1. Against whom did Amaziah want to fight?

2. Whom did he hire to go with him to battle?

3. Who told Amaziah that God was not with Israel?

4. How much did Amaziah pay for Israel's help?

5. What did Amaziah bring back from the Edomites?

Important Truths:

It is always better to listen to the man of God.

The best defense is God.

Money cannot fix your problems.

Marvelously Helped
II Chronicles 26:15-17
(Study: II Chronicles 26:1-23)

Uzziah was sixteen years old when he became king of Judah, and did right in the sight of the Lord. He sought God in the days of the prophet Zechariah and the Lord made him to prosper. God gave him victory over the Philistines, the Arabians, and the Ammonites. He built towers, digged wells, had much cattle, and a large army. God blessed and helped Uzziah tremendously because he sought the Lord. The Bible says, "But when he was strong, his heart became lifted up" and he went into the house of the Lord where only the priests were supposed to go. He was met and reproved by Azariah and eighty other priests entering the sanctuary. Uzziah became angry with the priests, and God smote him with leprosy.

---

1. How old was Uzziah when he became king?

2. Uzziah sought God in the days of what prophet?

3. Why was Uzziah marvelously helped?

4. When did Uzziah's heart become lifted up?

5. Why did the priest Azariah, reprove King Uzziah?

Important Truths:

God helps those who seek Him.

Don't get too big for your own good.

It does not pay to get mad at the man of God.

Adding More to Our Sins
II Chronicles 28:13-15
(Study: II Chronicles 28:1-27)

Ahaz was the king of Judah and did not do that which was right in the sight of the Lord. He did evil things such as: making images of Baalim, burning his children as sacrifices to false gods, and walking in the ways of the kings of Israel. God punished Ahaz and all Judah by allowing the king of Israel to slaughter 120,000 of them and take 200,000 of them captive. When the men of war took the captives back to Samaria, they were met by the prophet Oded, who reminded them that Israel had sins of their own against the Lord. Then certain heads of the people refused to allow the men of war to bring in the captives and said if they did so, they would be adding sin to the sins they had already committed.

1. Who was the king of Judah?

2. What sins had he committed?

3. How many of Judah were taken captive?

4. Who took them captive?

5. What prophet reproved Israel's army?

Important Truths:

We should not test God's mercy by sinning more.

God sometimes uses people to chasten us.

The way of the transgressor is hard.

Sanctify Yourself
II Chronicles 29:5-7
(Study: II Chronicles 29:1-36)

Hezekiah became king of Judah and did that which was right in the sight of the Lord. Ahaz his father, did evil in God's sight, and while he was king, he shut the doors of the house of the Lord. In the first month of the first year of his reign, Hezekiah reopened the house of the Lord, and called together the priests and Levites. Hezekiah told them to sanctify themselves and the house of God. His father had trashed the house of the Lord and it needed to be cleaned out. Before there could be a temple cleansing, there had to be a people cleansing. Hezekiah reminded the priests and Levites that the reason for Judah's trouble was because the wrath of the Lord was upon them. The Levites were God's chosen tribe and cleansing had to start with them.

---

1. Which king did right in the sight of the Lord?

2. Which king did evil in the sight of the Lord?

3. What did Hezekiah do as soon as he became king?

4. Whom did Hezekiah tell to cleanse themselves?

5. Who did Hezekiah say turned their backs on God?

Important Truths:

When returning to God, go back to church.

God's people ought to live a sanctified life.

We can break the chains of generational sins.

When Not to Laugh
II Chronicles 30:9-11
(Study: II Chronicles 30:1-27)

When Hezekiah became king of Judah, there was a spiritual revival. Hezekiah reopened the house of the Lord and encouraged returning to God. Hezekiah sent a proclamation throughout all Judah and Israel that people should come to Jerusalem to keep the Passover unto the Lord. At this time, Israel had already gone into captivity under the Assyrians, but the land of Judah had not. The remnant that was left throughout Israel was invited for the Passover as a way to return unto God. Unfortunately, when they received the invitation, there were some that laughed and mocked at returning to God. There were some, however, that humbled themselves and came to Jerusalem. Their obedience brought great joy and answered prayer.

1. Who was said to be gracious and merciful?

2. What did Hezekiah encourage the people to do?

3. What did Hezekiah want to keep at Jerusalem?

4. Who had already taken Israel into captivity?

5. Some of Israel's remnant laughed at what?

Important Truths:

God's invitation to return is to all His children.

Not everyone chooses to return.

Returning to God can bring joy and answered prayer.

Take Care of God's Men
II Chronicles 31:4-6
(Study: II Chronicles 31:1-21)

Hezekiah's father, Ahaz, had closed the doors of the house of the Lord during his evil reign. When Hezekiah became king, he sought the Lord and reinstituted temple worship. He appointed the priests and Levites to minister before the Lord and to give thanks and praise Him. Hezekiah gave offerings of his own substance, and then commanded the people to give their tithes and offerings so that the priests and Levites "might be encouraged in the law of the LORD." The people gave and there was an abundance. Hezekiah questioned why there was so much and Azariah the chief priest said, "we have had enough to eat, and have left plenty: for the LORD hath blessed his people."

1. What did Hezekiah reinstitute?

2. What was the portion commanded for the Levites?

3. Who was appointed to minister before the Lord?

4. The tithe encouraged the priest in what?

5. What priest said, "the LORD hath blessed his people?"

Important Truths:

God blesses those who give tithes and offerings.

The tithe can be an encouragement to God's men.

Leadership should tithe to be an example of obedience.

More with God
II Chronicles 32:6-8
(Study: II Chronicles 32:1-23)

Hezekiah, king of Judah, sought the Lord and God made him to prosper. Sennacherib, king of Assyria came up against Hezekiah to take Jerusalem, the capitol of Judah. Hezekiah prepared for the siege by building up the wall and making more weapons for a war. Then he went out to speak to the captains over the people and told them to be courageous, because there were more with them than with Assyria because they had the Lord. The people rested themselves on the words of their king and trusted the Lord. Hezekiah prayed, along with Isaiah the prophet, for deliverance, and God heard their prayer. The Lord sent an angel which destroyed all the mighty men and leaders of the Assyrian army. Sennacherib returned home only to be killed by his sons.

---

1. What was the capital of Judah?

2. Who was the king of Assyria?

3. Who did Hezekiah tell to be courageous?

4. What did Hezekiah say was with the Assyrians?

5. Who along with Hezekiah prayed for deliverance?

Important Truths:

We should follow the leader as he follows God.

We must prepare for war, but trust God for victory.

Leadership should point people to God.

Forgotten Benefit
II Chronicles 32:24-26
(Study: II Chronicles 32:24-33)

Hezekiah was truly blessed by God. God had given him riches and honor, flocks and herds in abundance, and victories in battle. Hezekiah even was sick unto death, and the Lord healed him and gave him another fifteen years to live. Hezekiah prospered in all his works because he sought God. Hezekiah soon forgot all that God had done for him, and let the pride of his heart get the best of him. God's wrath was upon him for his sin, and He was about to bring judgement. Hezekiah then humbled himself, and the Lord postponed his punishment until after his reign. Hezekiah was a good king and was honored at his death for his accomplishments, but because of pride and forgetting God, the kingdom would cease to have such peace and success!

1. What had God given Hezekiah?

2. How many years did God extend Hezekiah's life?

3. Why did Hezekiah prosper in all his works?

4. What caused Hezekiah to forget God's goodness?

5. Why did God postpone His judgment on Hezekiah?

> **Important Truths:**
>
> Fullness allows for forgetfulness.
>
> We should deflect praise to the real source.
>
> Pride erases the memory of what God has done.

Then Manasseh Knew God
II Chronicles 33:11-13
(Study: II Chronicles 33:1-25)

Hezekiah, a good king of Judah, had a son named Manasseh. Manasseh did evil in the sight of the Lord like unto the abominations of the heathen. He made altars for Baalim, worshipped the host of heaven, sacrificed his children in the fire to false gods, and set up an idol in the house of God. Manasseh caused Judah to follow his wicked ways. When the Lord sent warnings and reproof to them, they would not listen. So the Lord sent the Assyrians to take Manasseh captive to Babylon. It was while Manasseh was in affliction that he called out to God and humbled himself. The Lord heard his prayer and brought him again to Jerusalem as king. Manasseh knew then that the Lord was God and he turned from his wickedness to serve Him.

1. Who was Manasseh's father?

2. What are some of the evil things Manasseh did?

3. Who else did Manasseh cause to do evil?

4. Whom did the Lord send to punish Manasseh?

5. What caused Manasseh to seek God?

Important Truths:

Godly fathers do not always produce godly children.

Affliction has a way of making us seek God.

God is merciful to repentant sinners.

When He Was Young
II Chronicles 34:3-5
(Study: II Chronicles 34:1-33)

Josiah became king of Judah when he was only eight years old. His father Amon was not a good king, but Josiah did that which was right in the sight of the Lord. When he was only sixteen years old he began to seek after God. At age twenty, he began to purge the land of Judah of all its graven images. When he was twenty-six years old, he had the house of the Lord repaired. During its repair, they found the Book of the Law of the Lord and brought it to Josiah. After reading the Book, Josiah rent his clothes and began to weep because he knew that Israel and Judah were under the curse of God for forsaking Him. God saw how Josiah humbled himself at the reading of the Book and promised that he would die in peace and not see the evil to come.

1. How old was Josiah when he became king?

2. What did Josiah do at age sixteen?

3. What did Josiah do at age twenty?

4. What did Josiah do at age twenty-six?

5. What was found in the house of the Lord?

Important Truths:

There are young people who still seek God.

Our sense of sin is measured by our nearness to God.

The Book should be found, read, and practiced.

Meddling with God
II Chronicles 35:20-22
(Study: II Chronicles 35:1-27)

Josiah was a good king of Judah. He sought the Lord, put away idols, repaired the temple, and kept the Passover. After all this, Josiah put his nose where it did not belong. Necho, king of Egypt came to the river Euphrates to fight against the king of Assyria. Josiah went out to fight against Necho, even though the king of Egypt, was not against Josiah, but was fighting against the king of Assyria. Necho told Josiah to forbear meddling with God, because God told Necho to fight against the king of Assyria. Josiah would not listen and was shot by the archers in the valley of Megiddo. Josiah died and the prophet Jeremiah lamented and all Judah and Jerusalem mourned at his death.

---

1. What are some good things that Josiah did?

2. Who was the king of Egypt?

3. Against whom was the king of Egypt fighting?

4. Who commanded the king of Egypt to go to war?

5. What prophet mourned Josiah's death?

Important Truths:

Sometimes good men do dumb things.

Minding your own business will keep you from trouble.

Let God pick your battles.

No Remedy
II Chronicles 36:15-17
(Study: II Chronicles 36:1-23)

Israel was the northern kingdom that went into captivity under the Assyrians. Judah was the southern kingdom that later went into captivity under the Babylonians. Zedekiah was the last king to rule Judah before being taken by Nebuchadnezzar, king of Babylon. God sent his prophet Jeremiah to reprove Zedekiah, but he would not humble himself and listen to God's man. The children of Judah got to a place of no remedy, when they mocked God's messengers, despised His Words, and misused His prophets. When they reached this point, God allowed them to be destroyed. The house of God was burned, the wall of Jerusalem was broken down, and the remnant was taken into captivity.

1. Who went into captivity under the Assyrians?

2. Who went into captivity under the Babylonians?

3. Who was the last king to rule over Judah?

4. What prophet did God send to reprove Judah?

5. What did God do because He had compassion on His people?

Important Truths:

A disregard of God's reproof brings judgment.

No remedy is a result of refusing the cure.

Pride causes us to refuse reproof.

Who Will Volunteer to Go
Ezra 1:3-5
(Study: Ezra 1:1-2:70)

After Israel was in captivity seventy years in Babylon, God stirred up the spirit of King Cyrus to send back those who would go, to rebuild the house of God in Jerusalem. He forced no one to go, but simply asked for those who would be willing to go. Cyrus also encouraged those who did not go, to be willing to help those who did. So God stirred up a remnant of almost 50,000 people to go back to Jerusalem to rebuild the house of the Lord. King Cyrus even gave to Sheshbazzar, a prince of Judah, all the vessels that Nebuchadnezzar had brought to Babylon when he destroyed Jerusalem, so they could be put back in the house of God upon their return.

---

1. How long was Judah in captivity?

2. What king did God stir up to send Israel back to Jerusalem?

3. About how many went back to Jerusalem?

4. What prince of Judah took back the temple vessels?

5. Those who did not go back were asked to do what?

> **Important Truths:**
>
> God can use anyone to accomplish His will.
>
> God is looking for volunteers.
>
> Not everyone will volunteer to serve.

Those Who Frustrate Us
Ezra 4:4-6
(Study: Ezra 4:1-24)

The returning remnant of Jews that came from Babylon to Jerusalem was met with resistance from the people who inhabited their land while in captivity. These adversaries did not want the Jews to rebuild the temple. These enemies first tried to stop them by infiltration, and said they wanted to build with them, which Zerubbabel refused. Then they tried frustrating their purpose by causing them trouble. Then they tried accusation. They wrote a letter to Artaxerxes, the new king in Babylon, saying that if the Jews finished building the house of God and set up the walls in Jerusalem, that they would not pay taxes or follow their custom. Artaxerxes believed their lies and commanded that they cause the Jews to stop building immediately.

---

1. What were the Jews trying to build?

2. Who refused the adversaries' help in building?

3. The adversaries sent a letter of accusation to whom?

4. What did the adversaries do first to stop the Jews?

5. Who was hired to frustrate the Jews?

Important Truths:

Infiltration is an enemy tactic.

Frustration is an enemy practice.

Accusation is an enemy plan.

The House Was Finished
Ezra 6:14-16
(Study: Ezra 5:1-6:22)

The enemies of Israel were able to stop the Jews from building the house of God by order of King Artaxerxes. After a time and through the prophesying of Haggai and Zechariah, the people began to build again. They were confronted by the governor of the region and asked, "Who hath commanded you to build this house?" The eye of God was upon them and they could not cause them to cease, so they sent a letter to King Darius in Babylon to ask what should be done. Darius responded, to "let the work of this house of God alone" and to give them money for the advancement of it. The Jews finished building the house of the Lord, and rejoiced that God had turned the heart of the king toward them and strengthened their hands in the work.

1. Which king told the Jews to stop building?

2. Which prophets told the Jews to start building?

3. Who confronted the Jews because of building?

4. Which king gave permission to keep building?

5. Who gave money for the Jews to build?

Important Truths:

Listen to God's man.

The king's heart is in the hand of the Lord.

Finish what God has led you to start.

A Letter from the King
Ezra 7:26-28
(Study: Ezra 7:1-28)

Ezra was a priest that "prepared his heart to seek the law of the LORD, and to do it, and to teach in Israel statutes and judgments." Ezra came from Babylon with a second group to establish temple worship. Ezra had the approval of Artaxerxes the king who wrote a letter to help him. In the letter, the king said that Ezra was sent by the king, and that the king had given for the house of God in Jerusalem, and that others should give also. It would take Ezra and his company four months to get from Babylon to Jerusalem. God's hand was upon Ezra for good, for which he had safety, money, and help, to beautify the house of the Lord. Ezra praised the Lord for putting in the heart of Artaxerxes to give and to help with the house of God.

1. What position did Ezra hold?

2. What did Ezra prepare his heart to do?

3. Who wrote a letter of approval for Ezra?

4. How long of a trip was it from Babylon to Jerusalem?

5. Ezra was strengthened as what was upon him?

Important Truths:

God can use unsaved people to perform His will.

A man with God's hand on him can accomplish much.

Seek, do, and teach God's law.

The Hand of Our God
Ezra 8:21-23
(Study: Ezra 8:1-36)

Ezra received a letter of commission from King Artaxerxes to take a group of Jews from Babylon to Jerusalem to establish temple worship and beautify the house of God. Ezra gathered those who would go back of their own free will and noticed there were no Levites to minister in the temple. He sent word back into the city and two hundred and sixty men came to help serve in the house of God. As Ezra prepared to leave for Jerusalem, he stopped to pray and fast, to ask God for direction and protection for their trip. God put his hand on Ezra and his company as they took their four month journey and delivered them from enemies along the way. It was evident that the money, personnel, and safety was the hand of God.

---

1. What group of people did Ezra ask to go with him?

2. How many came to help serve in the house of God?

3. What did Ezra stop and do before he left?

4. For what was Ezra ashamed to ask the king?

5. How long was Ezra's journey?

Important Truths:

God's hand can be one of direction and protection.

Sometimes people just have to be asked to help.

The hand of God is on all for good that seek Him.

Married to Unbelievers
Ezra 9:1-3
(Study: Ezra 9:1-10:44)

Once Ezra the priest arrived in Jerusalem, the princes came to him and told him how the people of Israel had taken spouses from the people of the land and were doing their abominations. Ezra was astonished at the people's sin and gathered that night with those who trembled at God's Word. Ezra confessed to the Lord Israel's sin, and recognized that God had punished them less than they deserve. The people who heard Ezra's prayer said they would like to make a covenant with God to put away the strange wives. In three days, all the children of the captivity gathered to Jerusalem to perform the oath of separation. However, those who had taken spouses from the heathen were many, and it took three months for separation to be complete.

1. Who told Ezra of the people's sin?

2. Who were the chief offenders in marrying the heathen?

3. What was Ezra's reaction when hearing of their sin?

4. The people made a covenant with God to do what?

5. How long did it take to make a separation?

Important Truths:

A Christian should not marry an unbeliever.

Unbelievers can cause believers to act like unbelievers.

God can forgive any sin.

Let Us Rise and Build
Nehemiah 2:17-19
(Study: Nehemiah 1:1-2:20)

Nehemiah was a Jew living in Babylon and working as the king's cupbearer. One day, he had some visitors come from Jerusalem who told him that the remnant living there was in great affliction and that the walls of Jerusalem were broken down. Nehemiah was broken-hearted about it and asked the Lord what he could do about it. The king soon noticed a change in Nehemiah's countenance and asked what was wrong. Nehemiah told him of the state of Jerusalem and asked if the king would send him back to build it back up. The king said, "yes," and also gave him letters for timber and soldiers for safety. When Nehemiah arrived the people united with him and said, "Let us rise up and build."

---

1. What occupation did Nehemiah have in Babylon?

2. What was Nehemiah broken-hearted about?

3. What two things did the king give to Nehemiah?

4. What did Nehemiah want to build?

5. Who laughed at the Jews' desire to build the wall?

Important Truths:

One person with desire can get something started.

There are those who will throw water on your fire.

Many hands make light work.

A Mind to Work
Nehemiah 4:4-6
(Study: Nehemiah 4:1-23)

Nehemiah and the children of Israel began building the wall of Jerusalem. All kinds of people came out to help build the wall: priests and Levites, goldsmiths, apothecaries, and merchants. Yet, it did not take long for them to receive opposition from Sanballat and Tobiah. They began to ridicule and conspire to come fight against the Israelites in Jerusalem to hinder it. Nehemiah charged them to not be afraid, to remember the Lord, and to fight for their families. Because the people had a mind to work, they continued building. With one hand they worked on the wall and with the other they held a weapon to fight if necessary. Because of the leadership and prayers of Nehemiah, the people kept moving forward, and the wall continued to go up.

---

1. What kind of people helped build the wall?

2. Who opposed the Jews in building?

3. What did Nehemiah charge the people to do?

4. What did the people do with each hand?

5. Who kept the people moving forward?

Important Truths:

Some things are worth fighting for.

The enemy wants to keep us from building.

Work starts in the mind.

The Wall Was Finished
Nehemiah 6:14-16
(Study: Nehemiah 6:1-19)

Nehemiah's goal was to rebuild the wall of Jerusalem and he finished it with the help of the people in fifty-two days. The closer he got to finishing, the more their enemies put the pressure on them to quit. They tried using false accusations, and said that Nehemiah was trying to make himself king over Jerusalem. Then they used temptation by trying to tempt Nehemiah to do wrong by hiding himself in the temple where only priests were supposed to go. When both of those did not work, they tried to put them all in fear. When the wall was finished, Nehemiah's enemies realized that the work was wrought of God!

---

1. How long did it take to finish building the wall?

2. What three things did the enemies of Nehemiah do to try to get him to stop building the wall?

3. What did the enemy try to tempt Nehemiah to do?

4. What did the enemies realize when it was finished?

5. What prophetess tried to put Nehemiah in fear?

> **Important Truths:**
>
> Great things are possible if we just keep at it.
>
> Finishing is a testimony to all of what God can do.
>
> Satan will try different things to stop God's work.

Attentive to the Book
Nehemiah 8:1-3
(Study: Nehemiah 8:1-18)

The people of Jerusalem gathered together as one man into the street and asked Ezra to bring the Book of the Law and read it unto them. Men, women, and those that could understand, came together from morning until midday and were attentive to the Book. Ezra "read in the book in the law of God distinctly, and gave the sense, and caused them to understand the reading." While Ezra read from God's Word the people stood with their faces to the ground and wept and worshipped God. The people went their way with joy because they understood the words that were declared unto them. Some came back the next day so Ezra could read and help them to understand more.

---

1. What Book did Ezra bring to the meeting?

2. Who came and were attentive to the Book?

3. How did Ezra cause the people to understand?

4. What did the people do while Ezra read the Book?

5. Why did the people leave with joy?

Important Truths:

The Bible changes lives.

We use the Bible to worship the Lord.

The Bible can bring both joy and sorrow.

Vashti Refused
Esther 1:10-12
(Study: Esther 1:1-22)

King Ahasuerus was the king over 127 provinces, from India to Ethiopia. In the third year of his reign, he made a feast in Shushan, the palace. Ahasuerus entertained the men and Vashti the queen made a feast for the women. The king was intoxicated with wine and called for Vashti to come and "shew the people and princes her beauty: for she was fair to look on." However, Vashti refused to come at the king's commandment, which made him very angry. One of the princes of the kingdom named Memucan, recommended to the king to take the queenship away from Vashti for disobeying the king. Vashti lost her position, but she kept her virtue by not making her body a spectacle to others.

1. Over how many provinces did Ahasuerus reign?

2. Where was the palace of Ahasuerus?

3. What did Ahasuerus want Vashti to show?

4. Which prince recommended to remove Vashti as queen?

5. Vashti lost her position, but kept what?

Important Truths:

Sometimes you will have to say no, to do right.

Doing right is not gauged by the outcome.

Alcohol makes you do stupid things.

Haman, Enemy of the Jews
Esther 3:8-10
(Study: Esther 3:1-15)

Ahasuerus, the king of the Persian empire, promoted Haman to be above all the other princes and caused people to reverence him. Mordecai, the Jew, gave Haman no such recognition and Haman became angry toward Mordecai because of it. Haman wanted to hurt Mordecai and also his entire race of people. When Haman found out that Mordecai was a Jew, he went to the king and lied about the Jewish people and asked if he could kill them. The king, not knowing Haman's intent, granted him his request. At that time, the first month of the year, he made a decree in the writing of the king that in the twelfth month every Jew could be killed, and their things taken. This writing was sent to every province for the enemies of the Jews to be ready.

---

1. Who was the king of the Persian empire?

2. Why did Haman become angry with Mordecai?

3. What group of people did Haman want to kill?

4. In what month did Haman want them killed?

5. How much would Haman pay to have them killed?

> **Important Truths:**
>
> The Jews are God's chosen people.
>
> Pride was the root cause to destroy a nation.
>
> Anger will cause a person to do unthinkable things.

For Such a Time as This
Esther 4:14-16
(Study: Esther 4:1-10:3)

Haman, the Jew's enemy, convinced King Ahasuerus to destroy the Jews out of hatred for Mordecai. Mordecai was the uncle to Queen Esther, and he told her to go plead for her people. He reminded her that she became queen for such a time as this, to be an instrument to save her people. Esther fasted for three days, and then went before the king, and found favor in his eyes. King Ahasuerus asked Esther what her request was and it would be given her to half the kingdom. Esther asked for her life and the life of her people. Ahasuerus asked who presumed to kill her, and she said this wicked Haman. The king had Haman hung, and allowed the order to be given for the Jews to defend themselves.

1. Who was the Jews' enemy?

2. Who was uncle to Queen Esther?

3. How long did Esther fast before going to the king?

4. Who else did Esther ask to fast for her?

5. How did the king have Haman killed?

Important Truths:

Man's goings are of the Lord, and happen in His time.

We should plead for the salvation of others.

God always wins in the end.

Satan Attacks Job

Job 1:8-10
(Study: Job 1:1-2:10)

God gave us a book of the Bible to tell us the story of a man named Job. God gave the character description of Job twice to Satan. He said that Job was perfect, upright, one that feared God, and hated evil. Satan told God that the only reason Job feared Him was because He put a hedge about Job, his house, and all that he had. God gave Satan permission to touch all that he had, but not Job himself. Satan took away his wealth and ten children, but Job's response was "the LORD gave, and the LORD hath taken away; blessed be the name of the LORD." When Satan received permission to touch Job, but not take his life, he smote him with sore boils. "In all this did not Job sin with his lips."

1. How did God describe Job's character?

2. What three things did God put a hedge about?

3. What did Satan first take away from Job?

4. With what did Satan smite Job?

5. Who said there was none like Job in the earth?

Important Truths:

Satan has to have permission to do what he does.

God's hedge is one of blessing and protection.

The test of one's devotion comes under pressure.

He Knoweth the Way That I Take

Job 23:8-10
(Study: Job 23:1-17)

When all of the evil from Satan fell upon Job, then came his three friends to comfort him. Eliphaz, Bildad, and Zophar were miserable comforters. Instead of comforting Job, they accused him of being wicked, a liar, and an hypocrite. Most of the book of Job is filled with their accusations, and Job's rebuttals to retain his integrity. Job did not know why God was allowing all of the trouble in his life, but he knew that God was in control. Job said he did not know where God was, but that he knew that God knew where Job was. Job recognized that God was performing the thing appointed for him, and making his heart soft. During Job's sense of being alone, he said "I have esteemed the words of his mouth more than my necessary food."

1. Who were Job's three friends?

2. What three things did Job's friends accuse Job of being?

3. When did Job say he would come forth as gold?

4. What was more important to Job than food?

5. What would Job's trial do for his heart?

Important Truths:

God always knows what we are going through.

Sometimes friends can be miserable comforters.

During trouble, stay in the Bible.

God Turned It
Job 42:8-10
(Study: Job 42:1-17)

Job, under the temptation of Satan, lost his wealth, family, and health. Yet, through it all he did not curse God, or charge God foolishly. Job's three friends did not help him by telling him that his troubles were self-inflicted because of his own sin. Job went through months of pain and sorrow and still trusted the Lord to know what was best for him. In the end, God was not happy with Job's three friends and told them to go and have Job pray for them. When Job prayed for his friends, God turned Job's trial into a blessing. God blessed the latter end of Job more than his beginning by giving him twice as much as he had before. Job lived to be 140 years old, seeing four generations of his family.

---

1. What three things did Job lose under Satan's attack?

2. Why did Job's three friends say Job's trouble was self-inflicted?

3. When did God turn Job's trial into a blessing?

4. How much more did God give Job than before?

5. How old was Job when he died?

Important Truths:

It pays to trust God through trials.

Faith is not made sight, until the end.

Forgiveness releases us from our own captivity.

I Am Ready to Halt
Psalm 38:16-18
(Study: Psalm 38:1-22)

David is writing this Psalm of remembrance and makes the statement "I am ready to halt." David's great sin in life was committing adultery with Bathsheba. David's sin did not go unpunished. The baby died, his daughter was raped, his son was killed, and another son dethroned him. Yet, David went through much more than that. He describes the chastening hand of God as giving him no rest, pressing him sore, a heavy burden, sorrow, trouble, making him feeble and broken, and causing his strength to fail and him to mourn all the day long. God's punishment brought David to a place to acknowledge his sin and say, "I am ready to halt." David called on God and said, "Forsake me not, O LORD: O my God, be not far from me…Make haste to help me."

---

1. What was David's great sin in life?

2. What happened as a result of David's sin?

3. What did God's chastening hand do to David?

4. For what was David sorry?

5. What did David say he would declare?

Important Truths:

God both punishes and forgives His children.

Sin will cause a lot of trouble.

Halting from sin begins with being sorry for sin.

The Strange Woman
Proverbs 7:21-23
(Study: Proverbs 7:1-27)

Solomon was the wisest man to ever live, and "even him did outlandish women cause to sin" (Nehemiah 13:26). In his younger years, he had been warned about the dangers of the strange woman. On one occasion, he tells the story of a young man who was deceived and taken into immorality by the flattery and enticements of her. The strange woman had the attire of an harlot, the voice of flattery, and unashamed contact. She took away all fear by assuring the young man that her authority was out of town and would be gone for some time. He was set up as an ox for the slaughter. Her reputation is one that has wounded many and she has slain many by her immoral practices.

---

1. Who was the wisest man to live?

2. Who warned about the danger of strange women?

3. How did the strange woman force the young man?

4. What was the attire of the strange woman?

5. The young man was compared to what animal?

Important Truths:

Immoral living will either wound or slay you.

The wisest of men have been taken by immorality.

Immorality starts in the heart.

Here Am I
Isaiah 6:8-10
(Study: Isaiah 6:1-13)

The prophet Isaiah tells of his vision of the Lord in the year that the good King Uzziah died. When he saw God on His throne, his eyes were opened to see several other things. He saw himself as a sinner, he saw the need to go, and he saw the urgency of time to do something. In Isaiah's vision of God, he heard Him say, "Whom shall I send, and who will go for us?" Isaiah's answer to God's question was "Here am I; send me." Isaiah said he was willing and wanting to do what God needed. Isaiah went to the people of Israel and spoke God's message as He desired. Isaiah asked the Lord how long he wanted him to speak His message, and God said, "Until the cities be wasted without inhabitant."

---

1. Who had died when Isaiah saw his vision of God?

2. Where was God in Isaiah's vision?

3. How did Isaiah see himself, when he saw God?

4. What was Isaiah's answer to God's question?

5. How long was Isaiah to deliver God's message?

Important Truths:

When we see God, we will see our own sinfulness.

"Here am I," should be our response to God.

Giving people God's message will be a lifelong job.

You Are Just a Tool
Isaiah 10:13-15
(Study: Isaiah 10:5-19)

Isaiah, the prophet, begins to prophesy concerning the nation of Assyria. It was Assyria who would take the northern kingdom of Israel into captivity because of their idolatry. Assyria was God's tool of judgement, but Assyria did not know that. They, in their pride, thought all that they were able to do was because of their own strength and wisdom. God said, through Isaiah, that He would judge Assyria after He used them to punish Israel for their sins. God used the picture of Assyria being like an ax, saw, rod, or staff. He said that tools can do nothing without a person picking them up and using them. So it was with the nation of Assyria, God had used them to chasten his people.

---

1. Who prophesied concerning Assyria?

2. Why would Israel go into captivity?

3. God used what four tools to illustrate Assyria?

4. Who said, "By the strength of my hand I have done it, and by my wisdom?"

5. What is the only thing a tool can do?

Important Truths:

God will punish His own for their disobedience.

All of us are just tools to be used by God.

It is easy to forget that God is in control of all.

The Fall of Satan
Isaiah 14:12-14
(Study: Isaiah 14:9-17)

Within the prophecies of Isaiah, we get a glimpse of the short story of Satan's fall as an angel of God. Lucifer, as Satan was once called, was cast down by God Himself. Satan was full of wisdom and perfect in beauty (Ezekiel 28:12). However, Satan in his pride said five times "I will." He said he would exalt his throne above the stars of God, and be like the Most High. When his heart was lifted up because of his beauty, he was cast out of heaven with the third of the angels that had followed him. The end of the story is soon to happen as he will be cast into a lake of fire to "be tormented day and night for ever and ever" (Revelation 20:10).

---

1. Who prophesied of Satan's fall?

2. What was Satan's name when he was an angel of God?

3. Satan was full of what?

4. How many times did Satan say "I will"?

5. What will be the end of Satan?

Important Truths:

Pride has been the downfall of many.

Nobody will be higher than God!

Satan knows his time is limited.

Amend Your Ways
Jeremiah 7:1-3
(Study: Jeremiah 7:1-10:25)

Jeremiah, the prophet, was sent by God to stand at the gate of the temple to proclaim to those who would enter to worship that they should amend their ways and their doings. Jeremiah warned them that if they did so, that they could dwell peacefully in the land. Up to this point, they were living abominably and serving false gods, and then coming and worshipping in the temple. God reproved them for their backsliding, but not only did they not obey, but they would not receive correction. Jeremiah told them that being wise, mighty, and rich was not to be gloried in, but to glory in that they understand and know God. Sadly, even the pastors had stopped seeking the Lord and caused God's people to be scattered.

---

1. What prophet told Judah to amend her ways?

2. Where did the prophet speak?

3. What would God do if Judah amended her ways?

4. The prophet told them they should glory in what?

5. Who caused God's people to be scattered?

Important Truths:

Doing good things, does not erase bad living.

Take seriously the reproof of a man of God.

God delights in those who know Him.

Wearied with Running

Jeremiah 12:5-7
(Study: Jeremiah 11:1-12:17)

Jeremiah was God's man with God's message for Judah. He told them they were wrong for serving false gods and that God would judge them by having them taken into captivity. They not only rejected God's message, but they wanted to kill God's messenger. Jeremiah asked God, "Wherefore doth the way of the wicked prosper?" God knew that Jeremiah was bothered by their threats. He answered Jeremiah with a question, "If thou hast run with the footmen, and they have wearied thee, then how canst thou contend with horses?" God knew there would be bigger battles and more enemies that Jeremiah would come up against, as horses are larger and faster than footmen.

---

1. To whom did Jeremiah give God's message?

2. What did Jeremiah say they were doing wrong?

3. Who did God say dealt treacherously with Jeremiah?

4. What did Jeremiah ask God?

5. Besides footmen, what would Jeremiah have to contend with?

> **Important Truths:**
>
> Small tests prepare us for larger tests.
>
> God can give strength for the impossible.
>
> You are not alone when enemies come.

Profitable for Nothing
Jeremiah 13:5-7
(Study: Jeremiah 13:1-27)

God often had the prophet Jeremiah use illustrations to get His message across to Judah. This time God told Jeremiah to get a girdle and wear it around his waist and after some time to take it and put it under a rock by the River Euphrates. After many days, God told Jeremiah to go and get it. When Jeremiah went to get it, he found it marred and profitable for nothing. God used this girdle to show how Judah was marred and good for nothing because they walked after other gods, and refused to hear His words. God warned Judah that the only way to not go into captivity for forgetting Him and trusting in falsehood, was to humble themselves in the sight of God.

---

1. To whom was the prophet Jeremiah speaking?

2. What did God tell Jeremiah to wear?

3. Where was Jeremiah told to bury it?

4. Why did God say Judah was good for nothing?

5. What could change Judah from being good for nothing?

Important Truths:

Nearness to God has to be maintained.

Pride always separates you from God.

You cannot be profitable apart from God.

The Clay Made Again
Jeremiah 18:4-6
(Study: Jeremiah 18:1-19:15)

God again uses another illustration to speak to His people through the prophet Jeremiah. God told Jeremiah to go down to the potter's house and watch him make pottery. When Jeremiah arrived, he saw the potter molding a piece of clay that was marred in his hand. Instead of throwing it away, he made it into another vessel that seemed good to him. God told Jeremiah that this was a picture of Israel. If Israel would return to God and forsake their evil way, then God could make them new again. But Israel said, "There is no hope," and we will do our own evil way. The people did not like Jeremiah's message or his analogy to them being marred clay.

---

1. To whose house did God tell Jeremiah to go?

2. What was marred in the potter's hand?

3. What did God say was a picture of Israel?

4. Who said, "There is no hope"?

5. What did the people think of Jeremiah's message?

Important Truths:

God can fix a messed up life.

Being made over, starts with being made right.

There is always hope with God's help.

Penknife Christian

Jeremiah 36:22-24
(Study: Jeremiah 36:1-32)

God told Jeremiah to write in a roll of a book His words against Israel and Judah. Jehoiakim was the king of Judah at the time of Jeremiah's writing. Jeremiah wrote of all the evil that God intended to bring upon Judah for their sin, in hopes that they would return to God and be forgiven. Jeremiah had Baruch the scribe read the roll at the house of God for the people to hear. Some of the king's princes heard what was written and brought it before the king. As the king read the words of Jeremiah, he began to take his penknife and cut pieces out and throw them into the fireplace. By the time he was done, he had burned up the entire roll because he did not like what was prophesied against Judah for their sin.

---

1. What prophet spoke the words of God?

2. What scribe wrote down the words of God?

3. Who was the king of Judah?

4. Who brought the words of God before the king?

5. What did the king do with the Word of God?

> **Important Truths:**
>
> God's Word will always stand true.
>
> Not everyone will want or believe the Bible.
>
> Sin will keep you from wanting to hear the Bible.

Dissembled in Your Hearts
Jeremiah 42:19-21
(Study: Jeremiah 42:1-43:13)

Judah was taken into captivity under Nebuchadnezzar, king of Babylon, for their sin. He left a remnant in Jerusalem under the leadership of a man named Gedaliah. Unfortunately, he was assassinated and the remnant was afraid Nebuchadnezzar would come back and destroy the rest of them for it. They came to Jeremiah and asked him to get direction from God whether they should stay in Jerusalem or go to Egypt. They promised they would obey whatever God said to do. Yet, ten days later when God told Jeremiah that they should stay, they refused to do so. Jeremiah told them that even when they asked for God's direction, they had dissembled in their hearts about going to Egypt.

---

1. Where were the Israelites taken into captivity?

2. Who was assassinated as governor in Jerusalem?

3. From what prophet did the remnant seek advice?

4. What were the two options for the remnant?

5. Which option did the remnant take?

Important Truths:

God does not always answer the way we want.

Fear can cause us to make wrong decisions.

The world is not a good choice for help.

Whether They Hear or Forbear

Ezekiel 2:3-5
(Study: Ezekiel 2:1-3:27)

Ezekiel was a prophet that was taken into captivity and he prophesied to the whole house of Israel from Babylon. Ezekiel received a commission from God to be His watchman for Israel and give them warning from God. God knew that Israel would be rebellious and not listen, so he told Ezekiel three times, "whether they will hear, or whether they will forbear," give them warning from God. Ezekiel spake God's Word to the rebellious house of Israel and left the response, and the result in the Lord's hand. By doing what God said, their blood would not be required at his hand, but at the hand of those who refused the warning.

---

1. From where did Ezekiel prophesy?

2. To whom did Ezekiel prophesy?

3. What kind of house was Israel?

4. God said Israel was like what kind of children?

5. How many times did God tell Ezekiel, "whether they hear or forbear"?

> **Important Truths:**
>
> God has given us a people to whom we should give His message.
>
> We are not responsible for people's response to God's message.
>
> There will always be those who hear or forbear.

I Sought for a Man
Ezekiel 22:29-31
(Study: Ezekiel 22:1-31)

Ezekiel was the prophet to the whole house of Israel, and was prophesying from Babylon. The Lord spoke to Ezekiel concerning His people, and then Ezekiel delivered that message to the children of Israel in Babylon. On one such occasion, God spelled out all the sins of Israel that caused them to be taken in captivity. Then, He specifically talked about the backsliding and the sins of the prophets, priests, princes, and people. He told Ezekiel that He sought for a man among these groups to stand before Him for the land of Israel, but found none. Israel was consumed in God's wrath because not one person was willing to stand up for the land.

1. What prophet did God speak to about Israel?

2. Who vexed the poor and needy?

3. How many people did God find to stand up for the land before Him?

4. In what groups of people did He look for a man?

5. What did God recompense upon Israel's own head?

Important Truths:

One can make a difference for others.

Sin is the ruin of a nation.

Leadership should be the first to make a difference.

The Desire of Thine Eyes
Ezekiel 24:16-18
(Study: Ezekiel 24:15-27)

Ezekiel was God's prophet to the whole house of Israel. On many occasions, God would have him illustrate God's message to His people, but this time it would be on a more personal level. God would take away Ezekiel's wife, who was the desire of his eyes, as a sign to Israel. Ezekiel spake unto the people and that evening his wife died. The next morning he did not mourn over the death of his wife, but did as the Lord commanded him. The people asked why he did so, and Ezekiel told them that he was doing what they would be doing because of their sin. Ezekiel told them that they also would lose the desire of their eyes, both their wives and sons and daughters and not even mourn for their loss.

---

1. Who was the desire of the eyes of Ezekiel?

2. God said He would take Ezekiel's wife with a what?

3. What was Ezekiel not to do when his wife died?

4. What did Ezekiel do the next morning after his wife died?

5. What would the Israelites lose because of their sin?

Important Truths:

Family is the desire of our eyes.

God sometimes takes from us, to be a testimony to others.

Our love for God should be more than for family.

Daniel Purposed
Daniel 1:6-8
(Study: Daniel 1:1-21)

Daniel was a Jewish captive taken into Babylon by King Nebuchadnezzar. King Nebuchadnezzar took certain of the children of Israel into the palace to serve. He chose those who had had no blemish, were skillful in wisdom, were cunning in knowledge, and had an understanding of science, so that after three years they might stand before the king. Daniel was one of those chosen for such a test. But Daniel as a Jew, was not supposed to eat or drink what the king was offering as nourishment. He purposed that he would not defile himself with it, and requested from the prince that he might eat pulse and drink water. God brought Daniel into favor with the prince and he gave him his request.

---

1. Where was Daniel taken into captivity?

2. For what qualities was the king looking?

3. What did Daniel purpose in his heart not to do?

4. What did Daniel request to do?

5. Who brought Daniel into favor with the prince?

Important Truths:

We should purpose in our hearts to do right.

Request should come before refusal.

God can bring us into favor with unbelievers for our benefit.

The Fiery Furnace
Daniel 3:16-18
(Study: Daniel 3:1-30)

King Nebuchadnezzar of Babylon made an image of gold and brought together all the leadership of Babylon for the dedication of it. He then made a decree that when the people heard the music, they were supposed to bow down and worship the image, or be cast into a burning fiery furnace. There were certain Jews named Shadrach, Meshach, and Abednego, that would not bow to the king's idol. King Nebuchadnezzar warned them to worship his idol or be cast into the fiery furnace. They answered the king that their God was able to deliver them, but if not, they still would not serve his gods. Nebuchadnezzar cast them into the fire, but God delivered them from the flame. When they came out of the furnace, Nebuchadnezzar promoted them in Babylon.

1. Who was the king of Babylon?

2. What did he set up for people to worship?

3. What was the signal to bow and worship?

4. Who would not worship it?

5. What was the punishment for not worshipping it?

Important Truths:

There is no god like our God!

Serve God even if there is not deliverance.

Our tests become a testimony to others.

God Rules
Daniel 4:24-26
(Study: Daniel 4:1-37)

Nebuchadnezzar, the king of Babylon, had a dream and wanted to know the interpretation of it. He could not get anyone to interpret the dream except for Daniel. In his dream he saw a large tree with fair leaves, much fruit, and meat for all. He also heard a voice that said, "Hew down the tree…Nevertheless leave the stump." Daniel told Nebuchadnezzar that the tree was him, who had become strong, and that God decreed for him to be driven from men to be with the beasts of the field for seven years. The reason the stump was left in the dream was because Nebuchadnezzar would finally realize that God ruleth over the kingdoms of men and giveth it to whomsoever He will. He would then receive his kingdom back.

1. Who had a dream?

2. Who interpreted the dream?

3. What was cut down in his dream?

4. Nebuchadnezzar would be like a beast for how long?

5. When would Nebuchadnezzar get his kingdom back?

> **Important Truths:**
>
> Promotion and demotion come from the Lord.
>
> God is merciful even in His correction.
>
> We should heed warnings from the man of God.

Daniel in the Lion's Den
Daniel 6:20-22
(Study: Daniel 6:1-28)

King Darius set up an hundred and twenty princes to rule over the land and three presidents to preside over them. Daniel was the preferred president because he had an excellent spirit. The other presidents and princes became jealous of Daniel and sought an occasion against him, but could not find a fault with him. They tricked the king into signing a decree that no one could petition any God for thirty days except the king, or they would be cast into a den of lions. Daniel still prayed to God three times a day as he did before. The accusers of Daniel reported him to the king, and had him cast to the lions. God sent His angel to shut the lions' mouths, for which the king was exceeding glad. The king then had Daniel's accusers cast to the lions, which devoured them.

1. Who was the king of the land?

2. How many presidents and princes were ruling?

3. What did Daniel's enemies trick the king into doing?

4. How many times a day did Daniel pray?

5. What eventually happened to Daniel's accusers?

Important Truths:

Leadership likes those who have a good spirit.

Jealousy will come back to bite you.

Never stop doing what you know is right to do.

According to the Love of God
Hosea 3:1-3
(Study: Hosea 1:1-5:15)

Hosea was a prophet of God in Israel. The Lord used Hosea's marriage to illustrate God's relationship with the nation of Israel. Hosea took a wife named Gomer and they had children together. After some time, Gomer was unfaithful to Hosea, left him, and played the role of an harlot. Her actions caused her to end up being penniless, rejected, and sold as a slave. God told Hosea to love her anyway, and he went down to where she was being auctioned off, and he bought her. God said that Israel had done the same by leaving Him and serving false gods. Yet, God loved Israel and was willing to take the people back if they would forsake their idolatrous lovers and keep to Him.

---

1. Who did Hosea marry?

2. What would Hosea's marriage illustrate?

3. Gomer played the role of a what?

4. Gomer's actions caused her to be sold as a what?

5. What did Hosea pay to buy his wife back?

Important Truths:

God loves us even when we are unfaithful.

Each believer has been bought with a price.

The road to sin leads to heartache and loss.

The Lord Took Me

Amos 7:14-16
(Study: Amos 7:1-17)

Amos prophesied against the northern 10 tribes of Israel and their king, Jeroboam. At the time of his prophecies, Israel was serving two golden calves, one in Bethel and one in Dan. Amaziah, the priest in Bethel, told Amos to stop prophesying against the king and Israel for their sin, and go give his message in the land of Judah. Amos told him that he was not a prophet, but just a herdsman with a message from the Lord. The Lord took Amos from following sheep, to preaching His Word to Israel. Amos told Amaziah that he would die in a polluted land and that Israel would surely go into captivity. At the time of his prophecy, it did not seem possible, but years later, it came to pass.

1. Who did Amos prophesy against?

2. Who was the priest at Bethel?

3. What was Israel serving at Dan and Bethel?

4. Where did the priest tell Amos to go prophesy?

5. What did Amos do for a living?

Important Truths:

God can use anyone that is willing to speak for Him.

There will be resistance to God's message.

Judgement day is coming.

Are You Running

Jonah 1:3-5
(Study: Jonah 1:1-17)

Jonah was a Jew who was told by God to go to Nineveh, the Assyrian capital, and preach against it. Instead of going to Nineveh, Jonah tried to run from the presence of the Lord, and got on a ship to go the opposite way, to Tarshish. God sent a mighty wind that threatened to break the ship. The mariners on the ship told every man to pray to his god to spare their lives and found out that Jonah was running from his God and was the cause of the storm. They asked him what they should do, and Jonah said to throw him overboard. As soon as they did so, the sea stopped her raging and the men feared the Lord. As for Jonah, God prepared a whale to swallow him whole.

---

1. What city was the Assyrian capital?

2. To where did Jonah try to run?

3. What did God send to threaten the ship?

4. What was Jonah doing when the storm came?

5. What did the mariners do with Jonah?

Important Truths:

You cannot run from God.

God will ask us to do things we do not want to do.

Storms are sometimes self-inflicted.

Second Chances
Jonah 3:1-3
(Study: Jonah 2:1-3:10)

God told Jonah to go to Nineveh and preach against them for their wickedness, but instead, he took a ship the opposite direction to Tarshish. Jonah ended up being thrown overboard and swallowed by a whale. In the whale's belly, Jonah cried unto the Lord and acknowledged his sin of disobedience. The Lord spoke to the whale and it vomited Jonah out upon dry land. Then the Lord told Jonah a second time to go to Nineveh and preach what He would tell him. Jonah arrived after a day's journey and began to preach, "Yet forty days, and Nineveh shall be overthrown." The people of Nineveh believed God, cried unto Him, and turned from their evil way. God heard their prayer and did not destroy them.

1. Where did God tell Jonah to go and preach?

2. What happened to Jonah for running from God?

3. To what did God speak, to release Jonah?

4. What was Jonah's message to the Ninevites?

5. Why did God not destroy Nineveh?

Important Truths:

God is a great and merciful God!

God gives second chances to get right and do right.

God's Word can bring revival.

It Is Up to You
Jonah 4:1-3
(Study: Jonah 4:1-11)

Jonah preached unto Nineveh, "Yet forty days, and Nineveh shall be overthrown." His preaching sparked a citywide revival in the capital of Assyria, and they fasted and prayed for God's forgiveness. God forgave them and changed His mind about destroying them. Jonah was very angry that God was not going to destroy these Gentile Assyrians. God asked Jonah, "Doest thou well to be angry?" Jonah thought he was justified for his anger, but God reminded him that there were 120,000 people in that city that had no discernment. God wanted Jonah to have compassion on the Ninevites, but instead his prejudices caused him to hate instead of care.

---

1. What sparked a citywide revival in Nineveh?

2. Was Jonah happy about Nineveh's revival?

3. What did God ask Jonah?

4. How many people were in the city of Nineveh?

5. What did Jonah say he knew about God?

Important Truths:

God cares about people and so should we.

Compassion will change how we see people.

We do not do well to be angry with God.

Revive Thy Work
Habakkuk 3:1-3
(Study: Habakkuk 1:1-3:19)

Habakkuk was a prophet that prophesied during the years of the good king, Josiah. Habakkuk recognized and exposed Israel's sins of idolatry. The Lord told Habakkuk that he would raise up the Chaldeans to punish Israel for their sin, and that they would take them into captivity. Habakkuk wrote the Lord's words to Israel. Five times God said "woe" to Israel, which means sorrow or distress. Israel would undergo the chastening hand of God for their sin, and Habakkuk was the bearer of such news. After hearing God's pronouncement against Israel, Habakkuk prayed to God and said, "revive thy work...in wrath remember mercy."

1. During what king's reign did Habakkuk prophesy?

2. Who would God use to punish Israel for their sin?

3. What did God mean when He said "Woe" to Israel?

4. What did Habakkuk pray for God to send?

5. What did Habakkuk ask God to remember?

Important Truths:

We should pray for God to send revival to His people.

There is sorrow and distress to the disobedient.

Even under good leadership, there is a need of revival.

Consider Your Ways
Haggai 1:5-7
(Study: Haggai 1:1-2:23)

―――――― ∽ ――――――

Haggai was a prophet to the returning remnant that came back to Jerusalem after seventy years of captivity in Babylon. The Jews had begun to rebuild the house of God, but had to cease because their adversaries convinced King Artaxerxes that the Jews sought to rebel. Haggai encouraged the remnant, and spoke to them by the word of the Lord to keep building, and to consider their ways. He reminded them that they finished their houses, but had not completed the house of God. Because of their failure to build God's house, they were sowing much, but bringing in little. The remnant of the Jews obeyed the Lord by the preaching of Haggai and finished the house of God.

―――――― ∽ ――――――

1. To whom did Haggai prophesy?

2. What did the adversaries hinder them from doing?

3. What did the Jews finish, and what did they leave unfinished?

4. Into what were their wages being put?

5. What did Haggai tell the remnant to do?

Important Truths:

God's Word is the supreme law of the land.

Consider what the Lord is doing in your life.

The house of God should be taken seriously.

What Is Your Offering Like
Malachi 1:6-8
(Study: Malachi 1:1-14)

Malachi was God's messenger to the restored remnant in Jerusalem after the seventy years of captivity. By this time, the house of God was rebuilt and temple worship was restored. Malachi tells the people that their offering to God should be their best, and not a corrupt thing. The people were bringing their animal sacrifices as offerings to God, but they would be blind, lame, or sick animals. God told Israel that He took no delight in their offering and would not accept it. Just like they would not give damaged goods to their human authorities, neither should they give a corrupt sacrifice to God, their great King! God told Israel, cursed be the deceiver that sacrifices a corrupt thing.

---

1. Who was God's messenger to the Jews?

2. What did God say a son does for his father?

3. What was wrong with the people's offerings?

4. What was God's response to Israel's offering?

5. Who did God say would be cursed for sacrificing a corrupt thing?

Important Truths:

We should give God our best!

Giving and giving right are two different things.

God takes delight in right giving.